The Construction of Cromer Pier

Christopher Simpson

Grosvenor House
Publishing Limited

All rights reserved
Copyright © Christopher Simpson, 2025

The right of Christopher Simpson to be identified as
the author of this work has been asserted in accordance
with Section 78 of the Copyright, Designs and Patents Act 1988

The book cover is copyright to Christopher Simpson

This book is published by
Grosvenor House Publishing Ltd
Link House
140 The Broadway, Tolworth, Surrey, KT6 7HT.
www.grosvenorhousepublishing.co.uk

This book is sold subject to the conditions that it shall not, by way of
trade or otherwise, be lent, resold, hired out or otherwise circulated
without the author's or publisher's prior consent in any form of
binding or cover other than that in which it is published and
without a similar condition including this condition being
imposed on the subsequent purchaser.

A CIP record for this book
is available from the British Library

ISBN 978-1-83615-213-2

The Construction of Cromer Pier

Contents

Preface	v
View of Cromer from the sea	vi
Chapter One: 1897	1
Chapter Two: 1898	16
Chapter Three: 1899	41
Cromer Protection Act 1899	55
Chapter Three: 1899 (continued)	59
Chapter Four: 1900	70
Chapter Five: 1901	123
Chapter Six: Official opening day: Saturday 8th June 1901	144
Acknowledgements	164

The Illustrated Sporting and Dramatic News: Saturday 15th June 1901

THE NEW PROMENADE PIER AT CROMER.

Preface

For centuries the coastline around Cromer has suffered relentless erosion from the elements and during the mid 19th century this had become so problematic that the "Cromer Protection Act" was passed in 1845, which was specifically devised to fortify the town from further encroachment.

Under this Act a promenade sea wall was constructed and in 1846 a wooden jetty was opened. The responsibility of building and maintaining the jetty and sea defences was undertaken by the Cromer Protection Commissioners and they raised funds by levying and collecting rates from the local community.

During the following 50 years, Cromer and the surrounding area grew into a popular holiday destination and as the town developed, the Commissioners recognised that in addition to providing protection from coastal erosion, the jetty and promenades had themselves become tourist attractions.

The devastating storm, which began on Sunday 28th November 1897, swept along the east coast and severely damaged Cromer's seafront.

This reference book follows the events after the storm through to the official opening of Cromer's current pier in June 1901, using newspaper articles from across the country and the minutes of the meetings of the Cromer Protection Commissioners, which were published in local newspapers, arranged in chronological order and supplemented with original public notices and photographs.

The meetings are of the Cromer Protection Commissioners, unless otherwise stated.

The articles have been faithfully reproduced, however, due to the print quality of the source material and several inaccuracies contained within the original Victorian/Edwardian text, some minor amendments and corrections have been made where possible.

View of Cromer from the sea

**Supplement to the Norwich Mercury:
Saturday 22nd July 1899**

Eastern view

1 Cromer Lighthouse

2 Royal Links Hotel

3 Doctor's Steps

4 Coastguard

5 The Gangway/Beach House

Western view

6 The Red Lion Hotel

7 Bath Hotel/Hotel Metropole

8 Tucker's Hotel

9 Hotel de Paris

10 Grand Hotel

Chapter One – 1897

Eastern Daily Press: Tuesday 30th November 1897 (article 1)

On the North Norfolk coast, the storm raged with exceptional fury and great destructive force. It did far more damage than its great predecessor early in the year. The storm may be said to have begun about five o'clock on Sunday afternoon.

From then, for the next four and twenty hours, it continued with but little or no intermission. At first the wind was westerly, but it soon got to north-west, and then the sea began to make rapidly.

A fine effect was produced when from time to time the dark waste of waters was illuminated by the lightning's flash, but as the evening wore on these became less vivid.

With the advance of night, the wind increased in force, and long before the welcome dawn arrived had risen into a gale. By that time also the quiet, placid waves were seething seas of raging foam.

Between 9 and 11 the seas were running very high, and both at Cromer and Sheringham were at their best for grandeur no less than for destruction.

The Cromer Jetty suffered severely. A number of its iron stays were washed away, and this favourite marine promenade left but a wreck of its former self. It looks more like a dismasted (sic) schooner with sea-swept deck than the once, compact and sound little structure that for long has been the sport of storms.

For the many sightseers who thronged the cliffs above, and viewed from safe vantage ground the work of destruction below, the scene was one not soon erased from memory. Even from their high position they were not free from the spray of the angry billows.

Towards the east end of the Lower Esplanade, Beach House came in for a rough time. The house stands low, and right on to the sea front. Here the waves made merry with the windows and the wind with the chimney stacks. The occupants lost no time to quit a scene undergoing a second deluge.

The lower portion of the gangway – an extension of which has been in contemplation – is destroyed, and access to the Beach for carts made a matter of much difficulty.

Happily, the lifeboat slipway is none the worse for the storm, but a number of iron stanchions on the new Esplanade adjoining are swept clean away. The coastguards' boat, which is kept on the cliff near this spot, was only just rescued in time from sharing what might have proved a similar fate.

*Norfolk Museums Service, Cromer Museum, CRRMU : 2017.17.21
Storm damaged Cromer Jetty*

Eastern Daily Press: Tuesday 30th November 1897 (article 2)

Seldom have our sea-girt isles been swept by such a violent and desolating hurricane as that through which we have just passed. The havoc it has wrought can at present be only wildly guessed at, and it may be days before the whole extent of the mischief is known. Certain, however, we are of this, that the coast of East Anglia has not been fortunate enough to escape the full fury of the storm.

Our columns to-day bear melancholy witness to the ruin which has followed in its wake, and as we write, tidings are still being received of stranded ships and lost lives. Sunday night has indeed cast the shadow of death over many a fisherman's home.

Inland it was a terrible night. The shrieking of the wind as it swept through the leafless trees and round the corners of the streets, the crash of an occasional tile or slate as it fell from the roof top, and the rocking of the more exposed houses will long be remembered by their sleepless occupants.

But the weird noises of the night were absolutely innocuous in comparison with the awful experience endured by those whose lives were for the time being placed at the mercy of the storm-tossed sea.

It is to be hoped that the sudden fall of the barometer during the afternoon may have warned the more experienced seamen of the coming gale, and kept them to the comparative security of the roadstead, though even there their fragile craft could not have remained altogether unaffected by the violence of the storm. But the vessels in the sorest straits were those which, coming from a distant port, happened to be sailing at the time along our perilous coast.

A hapless fate has overtaken not a few, and driven them helplessly towards the angry surf. Though full particulars are wanting, it is stated that five vessels have gone ashore between Hasboro' and Bacton, and that many hands were drowned.

Three lives have certainly been lost at Bacton, and four more were only saved from a similar fate by the timely assistance rendered by the rocket brigade.

At Hemsby it is reported that a brig has run aground, and it is feared that all on board except a woman, who was brought ashore in a dying condition, have perished. A seaman has been washed up by the sea at Caister, and other bodies, it is stated, have been seen floating in the water. Even this list, long as it is, may not exhaust the death-roll along the Norfolk coast.

If there have been no lives lost on shore it is not because the hurricane has done less damage there than at sea. At Yarmouth the Beach Gardens have been inundated, the Britannia Pier damaged, and many houses, including the offices of the Board of Guardians, flooded.

At Lowestoft, the Denes have been absolutely submerged, and St. John's Church filled with water. Further north the sea wall at Sheringham has been practically demolished, the Jetty at Cromer crippled, while a gaping breach has been made in the sea bank near Burnham.

Such a disastrous gale as this has not visited this county since that Sunday in March, 1895, when trees by the thousand fell like ninepins before the blast.

The hurricane of that day, however, had spent its force in less than an hour. For nearly twenty-four hours has the present nor'-wester been blowing big guns.

*Norfolk Museums Service, Cromer Museum, CRRMU : 2008.5.3
Storm damaged Cromer Jetty from the beach*

Eastern Daily Press: Friday 3rd December 1897

There was a renewal of the gale at Cromer on Wednesday night. Early yesterday morning the ketch Hero, of Goole, with coal from Goole to London, came ashore about one hundred yards west of the Jetty and the crew of four taken off by the lifeboat.

About two o'clock the coastguard observed the vessel showing signals of distress, and at once called out the lifeboat and the rocket company.

At the time a very heavy gale was blowing from north-north-east, and when the vessel struck, Captain G. H. Wilson, and his three comrades were saved by the united efforts of the lifeboat and rocket brigade.

The latter soon established connection with the ship. As, however, those on her did not, as they acknowledge, fully understand the working of the life-saving apparatus, when the hawser was hauled on board they let go the whip, which resulted in delay.

The rescued men were taken to the Red Lion Hotel and everything done for their comfort. It appears that about midnight the vessel lost some of her sails, and for four hours the men were at the pumps.

Flares were displayed, and when the Cromer light was sighted the captain made for shore, he and one of the others being at the wheel. Up to last evening the vessel had shifted a little from her position, but as yet shows no signs of breaking up.

While engaged in work connected with the wreck, Mr. McArthur, chief officer of the coastguard, had the misfortune to lose the top part of the fore finger of his right hand. During yesterday morning a boat belonging to the S.S. Oporto of London was washed ashore near the break-water below the Grand Hotel. It was in a damaged condition.

Norfolk Museums Service, Cromer Museum, CRRMU : CP1819
The Hero on the west beach with the damaged jetty in the background

The Thetford and Watton Times:
Saturday 4th December 1897

CROMER JETTY AND CLIFFS PARTIALLY DEMOLISHED

The roughest weather was experienced at Cromer about 4 o'clock on Monday morning. A neap tide was running, but at high tide the waves swept over the Jetty sea wall and enveloped the Beach House and Bath Hotel in showers of spray.

At the Beach House the occupants had to clear out, and the furniture had to be removed, for the windows were smashed in and the walls washed about, while the wind smashed all the chimney pots and took away part of the roof.

Tons of cliffs were carried away, the tide being so high that it ran quite up to them.

Mr. Hoare's breakwater planking was smashed, the stone groyne being cracked the whole way down.

"Sailor" Allen's boat had been placed with the idea of safety on the Esplanade, but the waves swept quite over the stone wall and simply smashed it to pieces ..... the fishermen's boats in many instances were hauled up the steep cliffs.

Just before high tide the railings of the Jetty were broken, and shortly after two strips of ironwork supporting the end were bent like tin by a large wave, and the end of the Jetty was carried away.

One of the wooden piles also was gone, while that part of the structure built out from the wall was lifted off the piling time after time, and it is simply marvellous that it was not carried away.

The high tide of Monday night bade fair to complete the work of destruction.

Houses have been badly treated, and the parish church has part of its roof blown off.

*Norfolk Museums Service, Cromer Museum, CRRMU : 1982.24.12
Storm damaged jetty with the Hero in the background*

The Norfolk News (Second Sheet):
Saturday 11th December 1897

LAST DAYS OF THE CROMER JETTY
THE STRUCTURE DOOMED
A FORWARD MOVEMENT

An adjourned meeting of the Cromer Protection Commissioners was held on Wednesday, when the report of the Works Committee on the damage done to their property by the gale was received.

Mr. G. Breese presided, and the others present were the Rev. J. F. Sheldon, and Messrs. J. Newman, L. G. Burton, A. E. Jarvis, J. Lovelace, J. Riches, sen., H. Rust, G. Riches, jun., G. M. Bultitude, J. Bower, F. W. Rogers, T. Puxley, and R. A. Clarke.

The substance of an exhaustive report on the state of the Jetty was that, with the exception of the upper planking recently put down, the structure was in a rotten condition.

As to the west breakwater, there had been a considerable scour at the shore end owing to the overhanging cliffs, making it dangerous to extend the concrete portion of the breakwater.

The beacon at the sea end of the groyne required replacing. There had been considerable erosion of the cliffs from the foot of the west gangway to the parish boundary, no less than 15 ft. being washed away between the gangway and the breakwater.

The concrete portion of the east breakwater had again dropped, and the uppermost part of the timber for a space of about 15 ft. urgently required renewal, stay piles being forced outwards and some of the beams broken.

They recommended that this work should be done at an estimated cost of £45, and the fissure in concrete part filled up. The committee recommended that the exposed concrete part of the wall at the base of Mr. S. Hoare's cliffs should be faced with cement to an average depth of 3 ft.

The banks at the east end of the wall had been washed away, and a gap 100 feet long, 20 feet wide, and 4 feet deep, formed at the back of the wall.

The Beach being low the committee recommended that that part of the sea wall from Melbourne House breakwater to the west gangway should be pointed in cement; also that the wall between that groyne and the cart gangway should be treated the same, both above and below the timber bond to an average depth of 2 feet.

They recommended that as the culverts in the sea wall were exposed and a source of danger, they should be provided with iron flaps. New standards were required for the Red Lion steps. The rails had been saved, and could be replaced.

On the East Esplanade twelve new standards were required, and one standard to be repaired. They recommended that the new standards should have chamfered bases so as to give them more strength. On the West Esplanade a portion of the tar paving had been forced up there, and the grating was covered.

It was recommended that the grating should be brought up to the surface, and the paving made good. Also, that the tar paving under the steps leading to the west gangway for a space of 6 ft. square should be put right, and the railing and two top standards.

On the consideration of the Jetty report, Mr. Bower asked if the committee made any recommendations?

Mr. G. Riches, jun. – We were not instructed to make any; simply report as to its condition.

Mr. A. E. Jarvis – Any idea what repairs would cost?

Mr. G. Riches, jun. – Nails and spikes a considerable item. [Laughter.]

Mr. Bultitude – Would any iron rods screwed to it make it satisfactory for a time?

Mr. Newman – Iron rods no use, if the thing is rotten.

Mr. Bower – Are we inviting the public on to an unsound structure? The question was whether the Jetty was safe for a public resort. He thought it was not safe.

Rev. J. F. Sheldon thought that from the report it did not look at all a satisfactory thing to patch the Jetty up. He did not see much use in spending more time over it.

Mr. Burton would have it temporarily repaired.

Mr. G. Riches, jun., said it was useless to spend money on repairs. The piles were bad as well as the long beams that carry the planks. The Commissioners were not warranted in providing an unsafe place for public resort.

A resolution was then moved by Mr. H. Rust, and seconded by Mr. T. Puxley, that the Jetty be taken down.

Mr. Bower raised a point as to the borrowing powers of the Commissioners. He believed they had borrowed to the full extent allowed by their Act, which was now waste paper.

The Clerk said the Act of Parliament provided money, among other things, for the erection of a jetty. There was also a clause as to keeping these works in repair. They could not erect a new jetty under their present Act. If they wanted a new one, fresh powers would have to be applied for. But they had no money.

Mr. Bultitude moved, as an amendment to Mr. Rust's resolution, that the Jetty be left as it is, with the entrance barricaded. Mr. J. Riches, sen., seconded.

Mr. Bower asked if the old material would pay for the labour of taking it down.

The Rev. J. F. Sheldon thought they should bear in mind that the season was coming on, and that they could not leave the structure in that condition. Cromer would have to go forward, and he did not think the course suggested by the amendment was a wise one to adopt.

Mr. G. Riches, sen., said they should have to get more borrowing powers in order to do the necessary work of the town. He did not believe in putting that matter off year after year. They had but to look at the cliffs from the west to the east of the town to see how much immediate work was needed.

The Chairman thought Mr. Riches was travelling from the subject. They were considering what should be done with the Jetty.

Mr. G. Riches, jun. – What's the use of discussing if we have no money to spend on repairs?

The Chairman – Make a rate.

Mr. G. Riches, jun. – The whole thing might be carried through and the protection rate not increased one penny.

He did not think they would be losers, but that the whole parish would gain by it. He thought if they were to spend from £3,000 to £4,000 for the west gangway, and with another £7,000 to £8,000 erect a jetty and do other necessary work, the payment of interest, &c., on that £10,000 to £12,000 would but amount to about their present rate.

He thought the matter had been left in abeyance long enough.

There appeared a divergence of opinion with the District Council, but either one or the other would have to do something. The time for haggling about how to get the money had gone by. There was work decided on in connection with the Jetty breakwater that would mean £700 or £800 out of the year's rate.

He did not see why the rate should be 1s. 4d. in the £ if things were done properly.

Mr. Lovelace – Is it too late to apply for a new Act this year?

The Clerk – Yes, the 30th November was the last day. Now you cannot promote a Bill before November of next year.

Mr. J. Riches, jun. – For an urgent case can't we get special powers?

The Clerk had understood a Member of Parliament to say that for an urgent case they might get the standing orders put aside. He saw no chance of success, and besides they could not claim that the erection of a Jetty was a matter of urgency.

The Rev. J. F. Sheldon asked whether leaving the Jetty standing would be a source of danger to the breakwater.

Mr. G. Riches, jun., said they might take off the shore end of the Jetty, so people could not get on to it.

With this isolation treatment one or two members concurred.

The Rev. J. F. Sheldon thought if they cut off this end they might as well take it all down, for why save the remainder. On a vote being taken, only Mr. Breese, Mr. Bultitude, and Mr. J. Riches, sen., were found to support the amendment.

Mr. Rust's resolution in favour of removal was then adopted.

The Chairman – Now, then, what do you propose doing?

Mr. G. Riches, jun. – Put the Jetty up to auction.

Mr. Burton – And let the purchaser take it down at his own expense.

Mr. G. Riches, jun. – The Commissioners could take it down themselves. There were portions of it that would be useful.

Mr. F. W. Rogers – Where are you going to store it? [Laughter.]

Mr. Newman moved that the Jetty be sold by auction, the details to be left for the Works Committee to arrange. Mr. Burton seconded, and this was agreed to.

The rest of the Works Committee's report was then adopted on the motion of Mr. F. W. Rogers.

Mr. G. Riches, jun., then moved the appointment of a Special Committee to meet at an early date to discuss and report fully as to obtaining further powers for the protection of the town.

This was seconded by Mr. J. Riches, jun., and agreed to, and the following gentleman were appointed: – Messrs. A. E. Jarvis, G. Riches, jun., L. G. Burton, F. W. Rogers, and J. Bower.

THE CONSTRUCTION OF CROMER PIER

The Clerk read a letter from Mr. P. M. Lucas, St. Mary's, Cromer, who wrote that "Mr. Case, the engineer, had advised those contributing to the new groynes that it would be beneficial to the protection of the Lighthouse Hills if the planking on the Cromer east breakwater was removed down to the level of the beach on the windward or Cromer side. Mr. Case considered that the scour would be lessened on the eastern side without causing any damage on the Cromer side."

Mr. Rogers moved, and Mr. J. Riches, jun., seconded, that the Works Committee meet Mr. Case or his representative and report to the Board, but this was soon withdrawn and the Clerk instructed when acknowledging to state its contents should be considered at a future date.

Eastern Daily Press: Tuesday 21st December 1897

SALES BY AUCTION.

Sale by W. G. SANDFORD.

THIS DAY.

CROMER.

TO BUILDERS, CONTRACTORS, SPECULATORS, AND OTHERS.

SALE OF THE JETTY.

W. G. SANDFORD has been favoured with instructions from the Cromer Protection Commissioners to Sell by Auction on TUESDAY, DECEMBER 21st, 1897, in One Lot, as it now stands, the JETTY,

Viz., all the Memel Balks, Beams, Cross Beams, Ties, Stays, Braces, Deck Deals and Cladding, Top Railings, Stanchions, Seats, Scantling, &c.; also Iron Screw Piles, Iron Braces, Bolts, &c.

The Conditions under which the above structure is offered will be named at the time of Sale, which commences at 12·45 p.m., on the Bastion at the foot of the Jetty.

Convenient Trains arriving at Cromer Railway Station from Holt and North Walsham.

THE CONSTRUCTION OF CROMER PIER

*Norfolk Museums Service, Cromer Museum, CRRMU : 1979.32.1.6
The auction of Cromer Jetty on Tuesday, 21st December, 1897*

The Evening Star, Ipswich: Friday 24th December 1897

When one day we received the report of the sale of Cromer jetty we were curious as to the circumstances which gave rise to its being brought under the hammer, and the urgent conditions which applied to its removal. It is now explained that the sale was merely a sequel to the recent gale, and what was disposed of was only a remnant of the structure, most of the original having been "knocked down" by the wild seas of a few weeks ago.

It was a brave old wooden structure that had stood just 50 years, having been opened in 1846.

The whole of the jetty has to be removed and cleared away by January 31 to make room for a new pier. The first offer was £5, and at £40 it was knocked down to Mr. Isaacs, who owns the Britannia Pier at Yarmouth.

The Downham Market Gazette: Saturday 25th December 1897

Cromer Jetty, after its recent buffeting by the waves, has come to an untimely end.

On Tuesday Mr. W. G. Sandford, under instructions from the Protection Commissioners, offered the Jetty for sale by public auction.

Much interest was taken in the proceedings, which were, however, of a very brief duration.

The structure was offered in one lot, and by the conditions of sale the purchaser is obliged, under penalty, to have it removed by the end of January. Another condition is that the piles are to be cut off 4 feet below the present level of the Beach. Bidding began at £2, and the hammer went down at £40, the purchaser being a Mr. Isaacs.

The Norfolk Chronicle and Norwich Gazette: Saturday 25th December 1897

Cromer has lost its jetty. The remains of the battered structure have been disposed of for £40 to Mr. Isaacs, who is under contract to remove the ruin by the end of January. The inhabitants of Cromer have, therefore, for their most immediate consideration the reconstruction of their jetty.

What has done duty for a pier in the past has been a singularly insignificant and, compared with the structures which are provided by watering-places of less popularity than Cromer, a trumpery erection. So much so that I am inclined to doubt if the ruination of it has been altogether of the nature of a catastrophe to the town.

If there is one attraction more than another that appeals to every individual visitor to a seaside resort it is the pier, and there are few, if any, visitors to Cromer who will be found ready to aver that the erection which has hitherto satisfied the town is what they desire to see.

When the jetty was erected Cromer was a place of insignificance compared with what it is at the present time; and although its popularity has been secured, despite of this attraction being of so inadequate a nature, there can be no doubt that progress in the future will largely depend upon competition with other similar resorts.

It is, therefore, somewhat disconcerting to observe the lack of spirit which was evinced by some members of the Improvement Commissioners at their last meeting, when the subject of the pier was under discussion.

I think the people of Cromer are face to face with an opportunity of no mean proportions; to use an appropriate simile, here is a tide which taken at the flood will lead them on to fortune. Cromer is a place that is being boomed until there is danger of the inhabitants having their heads turned, and there is no reason why the great British public should not be invited to speculate upon the prospects of a really up-to-date pier as a financial investment, except that it would be far better for the towns people to do it themselves, and keep their little preserves in their own hands.

Chapter Two – 1898

**The Norfolk Chronicle and Norwich Gazette:
Saturday 8th January 1898**

At a meeting of the Protection Commissioners on Wednesday, Mr. G. Breese presided, and the Clerk reported a debit balance at the bank of £203 2/10. During the month rates to the amount of £316 3/6 had been collected. Mr. R. Allen's report of work done was received, and payment by him of £22 15/6 in wages confirmed. It was resolved to ask Messrs. Barclay, Limited, to allow an overdraft of £250 to the end of next December.

The Clerk reported that the jetty was sold for £40, and after deducting £2 16/6½ for expenses, and £2 2/ for his commission, Mr. W. G. Sandford, the auctioneer, has sent a cheque for £35 1/5½.

The Special Committee appointed to consider the question of obtaining further borrowing powers recommended "That all the Commissioners elected by the owners be individually requested to guarantee towards the cost of promoting a new Protection Act for Cromer, in the event of the same being applied for by the Commissioners in the present year."

The Clerk, in reply to questions as to the cost of such an Act, said it was impossible to state what it would be, as it depended on the opposition it received, but the probable cost of an unopposed Bill would be £500 or £600.

Mr. F. W. Rogers said that would mean a guarantee of £30 on the part of each of the twenty Commissioners. The Clerk said the money would not only have to be guaranteed, but a certain amount would have to be forthcoming to meet expenses as the Bill proceeded.

Mr. Rogers moved the adoption of the committee's recommendation. It seemed the only way to get to work. If the Commissioners were not prepared to take that matter up let someone else do so. The ex officio members were not asked, because under the new Act there would be none. Mr. J. Riches, jun., seconded.

Mr. Riches moved, and Mr. H. Rust seconded, as an amendment, that all owners be first consulted. Mr. Newman said if the public were not asked they might oppose the Bill. After further discussion the amendment was lost, and the resolution was then adopted.

Norfolk Museums Service, Cromer Museum, CRRMU : 2011.37.82
Cromer Jetty in the process of being demolished

Unidentified newspaper article (Cromer Museum)

Norfolk Museums Service, Cromer Museum, CRRMU : 2015.7.5

In Memoriam
CROMER JETTY DEMOLISHED JANUARY, 1898.

No! is it really gone? that friend of years long past!
That's weather'd many a storm, withstood the wintry blast;
Shall I never more be able, as so many times of old,
To stand upon its farthest point, while 'neath the breakers roll'd?

Look away across the ocean, with its billowy breast of foam,
And in fancy dwell on distant friends, who've left the good old home;
Enjoy the freshest breeze, away off from the land,
Trace out the rugged cliffs, along towards Overstrand?
Shall I never there view again that bright and cheery sight,
Gleaming out amidst the darkness, the rays of Cromer light?
Shall I never more, upward looking, see that massive old Church tower,
Or sit and read in summer for many a happy hour?
Will the visitors no longer up and down its distance walk,
Listen sometimes to the music, or enjoy a friendly talk?
There's nothing now along the front to catch the stranger's eye,
Tho' nothing else its well-known shape could in any sense supply.
What Fate is this that has decreed thy swift and heedless doom?
What hearts are there so hardened for pity make no room?
How long's the name "Protection" for "Destruction" been mistaken?
Has every happy memory of the past been now forsaken?
O friend of old! my mind goes back to many a happy scene,
To the Coronation feast in honour of our Queen;
When the tables groan'd upon thee, a glad and pretty sight,
When all who lived in Cromer to a welcome had a right.
Many a merry party have danced upon thy boards,
And doubtless hearts been fetter'd with love's enchanting chords;
With bright and loyal bunting they've often made thee gay,
But now those joyous scenes are forever done away.
I watch'd last year the breakers, but when storm had done its will,
Thy tough old form, though battered, was proudly standing still.
With only a little outlay they could have made thee strong again,
But all the links of memory were pleaded, but in vain!
Thou'rt gone from outward view, but my heart will not forget,
Thou friend of years, tho' parted, thou'rt living fragrant yet!

ANON.

The Norfolk Chronicle and Norwich Gazette:
Saturday 5th February 1898

A meeting of the Protection Commissioners was held on Wednesday, under the presidency of Mr. G. Breese. The Clerk reported a credit balance at the bank of £16 1/8, and that Messrs. Barclay, Limited, had consented to allow a £250 overdraft to the end of December.

The collector's statement showed that rates to the amount of £37 11/4 had been paid during the month.

The Works Committee reported having refused early in January a request from Mr. J. J. Isaacs, the purchaser of the Jetty, to extend the time for its removal, and also intimated in response to his inquiry that there was no chance of the Commissioners reconsidering the question of repairing and extending the structure. The committee reported with respect to the ketch Hero now on the beach, that after consultation with the Highways Committee of the Urban Council they had informed the owners of the ship of the serious danger she was to the Commissioners' works.

In calling upon them to remove her without delay, the owners were told they would be held responsible for damage done. The Clerk, in reply to questions, said the Commissioners had no power to compel the owners to remove the vessel. The report was adopted.

At the last meeting the Clerk was instructed to ascertain from each Commissioner if he would be willing to guarantee towards the cost of promoting a Bill in Parliament. The Clerk now reported that of the twenty members nine were willing, six had refused, and five had not yet answered. Mr. G. Riches, jun., asked how soon a meeting of property owners would be called to meet the Commissioners.

The Clerk thought that from an owner's point of view good notice should be given, but that the Commissioners would meet them as soon as they liked. Mr. A. E. Jarvis thought it would strengthen their case in asking the owners to back them up if none of the Commissioners were willing to become guarantors. Mr. J. Smith said that in case of strong opposition being shown they would withdraw their application for an Act. Mr. H. Rust held that had they gone to the owners first there would be no difficulty about a guarantee.

On the motion of Mr. R. A. Clarke, seconded by Mr. John Smith, it was resolved to have a meeting of owners on Wednesday, the 16th inst.

The Evening Star, Ipswich: Thursday 17th February 1898

A conference was held on Wednesday afternoon, at Cromer Town Hall, between the Protection Commissioners and the owners of property, to consider whether the former body should apply to Parliament for a Protection and Improvement Act for the town.

Mr. G. Riches, jun., presided over a fairly representative gathering, including Col. H. E. Winter, Rev. E. H. Savory, and Mr. T. W. Keith (Agent to the Bond-Cabbell estate). – The Chairman explained that the Commissioners had exhausted the borrowing powers, which were limited to £7,000, under the old Act, and the Commission which had the proposed new Act under consideration had drawn out a list of improvements needed with their approximate cost.

For the western extension, with promenade, the cost was estimated at £10,000; a pier, or jetty, £8,000; footing the present sea wall, £1,000; jetty breakwater, £1,000; eastern extension of wall, £2,000; east breakwater, £800; paying off old loan, £7,000; charges and other expenses, £2,000; total, £31,800. No maximum sum had, however, been fixed. Mr. Keith took it that they were considering a hypothetical case.

The whole thing depended upon whether the owners or Commissioners were prepared to guarantee the costs of the Bill. – In the course of further remarks, he said that undoubtedly the time had arrived for the amalgamation of representatives of the owners and the Council, a remark which was received with loud applause. – Mr. Bower moved, "That it was desirable that the Commissioners should apply for an Act to borrow money for protective and improvement work." – Mr. L. G. Burton seconded. – Mr. F. W. Rogers moved as an amendment, "That some scheme of amalgamation, if practicable, is preferable to the existence of two bodies." – The Rev. E. H. Savory seconded, and on being put to the meeting the amendment was carried by a substantial majority.

The Norfolk Chronicle and Norwich Gazette: Saturday 5th March 1898

A meeting of the Protection Commissioners was held on Wednesday, under the presidency of Mr. G. Breese. The Clerk reported a credit balance at the bank of £3 10/8, and that during the month rates to the amount of £18 3/11 had been collected.

The Works Committee were instructed to select suitable sites and obtain estimates for the erection of a couple of shelters. Mr. G. Riches, in inviting discussion on the resolution adopted at the recent meeting of owners at the Town Hall in favour of the amalgamation, thought it was a matter of doubt whether two or three who put their hands up were bona fide voters. On such a question as that before them he thought it should not be impossible to get an expression of opinion from each individual owner. Mr. Bower said the resolution was in no respect binding on the Commissioners, but was merely an expression of opinion on the part of the meeting.

As to amalgamation with the Council, he thought that body had already more work than it could do. The matter was of importance to the town, and he thought the protection of the place would be better seen to by the Commissioners than the Council. After much discussion, Mr. T. Puxley advocated all Commissioners becoming guarantors for the promotion of an Act, on the condition that they could withdraw if opposition was threatened. A great point in the discussion of the subject was how the rate would be affected by an amalgamation scheme.

He thought a ratepayers' meeting would favour the Commissioners retaining their position. Mr. A. E. Jarvis thought something should be done, especially as there seemed some misunderstanding among several members of the Council, and so far as he could see there was likely to be a split among them.

He would like each Commissioner to be again asked to guarantee towards the cost of a Bill. In the event of their agreeing to do so, he proposed they should next send a memorial to the owners for signature.

With the guarantee of both Commissioners and owners they could go forward, and when the new Council was elected, ask if they intended to oppose them. He concluded by moving a resolution to that effect, which was seconded by Mr. J. Riches, jun., and adopted.

Thirteen out of the fourteen Commissioners present put down their names as guarantors. Mr. J. Lovelace, having called attention to the need for more seating accommodation on the esplanade now that there is no jetty, Mr. G. Riches moved, and Mr. R. A. Clarke seconded, that the Works Committee obtain fifty seats at the same cost as those last purchased. This was agreed to.

Eastern Evening News: Thursday 24th March 1898

A strong northerly gale sprang up on the North Norfolk coast during yesterday.

At both Sheringham and Cromer the waves were washing the base of the cliffs an hour or two before high tide.

THE CONSTRUCTION OF CROMER PIER

As evening advanced, and the sea broke over the promenades at Cromer, the dismantled ketch Hero, anchored near the lifeboat house, was an object of interest to those on shore, as the unlucky craft was buffeted by wind and wave.

Not many vessels were seen in the offing during the day, but one going south appeared to experience much difficulty in getting round Cromer.

East Anglian Daily Times: Saturday 26th March 1898

Our Cromer correspondent writes: – A heavy gale from the north, veering round to N.-N.E. has been raging here since Thursday morning, sudden squalls of wind bringing terrible showers of hail and snow.

Not until midnight was the Hasbro' Lightship discernible, when the storm appeared to abate, but towards morning it became intense again, and has been raging all day.

The old wreck Hero, lying on the beach, was dashed up to the new Esplanade, and had her head smashed in against the slipway, and is now lying filled with water.

The fishermen are heavy sufferers, as about 200 crab pots were laid out on Wednesday, and are doubtless now smashed to pieces. Several dilapidated ones have been washed ashore.

The Daily Telegraph: Thursday 7th April 1898

CROMER

This Eastertide will witness a greater influx of visitors than has been the case for many years.

Princess Victoria of Wales has taken up her residence at Carrington-Villas, Lord Suffield's resort.

Visitors will notice a great loss to the town by the destruction of the jetty, but a year hence will probably see the commencement of a new and more ornamental structure. Meanwhile two shelters are to be erected upon the esplanades, while the old approach to the beach is to be transformed into a splendid carriage-way.

The Lowestoft Journal: Saturday 23rd April 1898

..... After refreshments the way is made seawards. Hereabouts a former familiar sight to visitors to Cromer is missing. The well-known Jetty is gone, and hardly a trace of it is left. It was carried away by the great storm on the 29th of last November. In the coming season there will be many who will miss this old structure. There are at present no signs of it being replaced.

Going in the direction of Overstrand many evidences are to be seen of the effects of the winter storms.

The Daily Telegraph: Friday 3rd June 1898

Cromer – The jetty, having been washed away in last November's gale, two spacious ornamental shelters are to be provided for the summer. This is a boon that will be greatly appreciated.

East Anglian Daily Times: Thursday 16th June 1898

The loss of the jetty that stood on the spur of the cliff, is not, however, a matter for very great regret. A new Act of Parliament is being applied for, and, when granted, a pier of much greater pretensions will be built, and will constitute an attraction that while the old jetty stood could not be provided.

After all, many of the claims of Cromer on popularity are of a negative nature.

There is no Spa such as Scarborough possesses, no jetty such as we find at Great Yarmouth, no Esplanade like that of Brighton, and, glorious as the beach is as a beach, there are none of those features usually associated with a seaside town.

Cromer is very polite and proper. It lives in an atmosphere of reserve and repose and restfulness.

The East London Advertiser: Saturday 18th June 1898

Cromer – One of the most delightful resorts on the shores of the North Sea, this healthy Norfolk town becomes more popular every year. There are no amusements to speak of. Visitors bathe in the morning (machines are plentiful) and cycle, drive, or golf in the afternoon, and there is, in the height of the season, a band generally playing in the evening on the esplanade; the old jetty has been demolished.

The beach is of clean, fine sand, washed by the tides twice daily. The scenery in the vicinity reminds one strongly of Devonshire – hill and valley, wooded slopes, lanes fringed with ferns and wild flowers.

There are good shops, the drainage is perfect, and the lodgings plentiful though not cheap. The Great Eastern runs express trains to Cromer, and the Great Northern and Midland Joint also run to Cromer-Beach. Distance from London 130 miles.

The Monmouthshire Beacon: Friday 15th July 1898

Visitors to Cromer often express surprise at finding the town without a jetty.

The Commissioners have now decided to apply to Parliament to borrow £50,000 for the purpose of erecting a pier and other works, and this time next year may see the commencement of the work.

Norfolk Museums Service, Cromer Museum, CRRMU : 1982.14.9
West beach – Saturday, 6th August, 1898

Eastern Evening News: Thursday 18th August 1898

The adjourned meeting of the Cromer Protection Commissioners was held yesterday at the Clerk's Office, Church Street, Mr. J. Riches in the chair.

The Special Committee with regard to the Protection Bill reported that the correspondence that had taken place between the Clerk and Messrs. Sharpe & Co., the Parliamentary agents, since the last meeting of the Commissioners had been read.

The agents point out that the proposal for constructing a pier and the engagement of a band out of the owners' rate might possibly be objected to by the Parliamentary Committee, although there was nothing to prevent the giving of such power if Parliament thought proper.

The committee expressed no opinion on the matter, but recommended a further adjournment of the Commissioners to Friday, 2nd September, to allow of more correspondence taking place with regard to it.

Mr. Jarvis thought that perhaps it might be possible to modify the clause objected to. The Clerk said it was only a matter of opinion whether there would be an objection to that part.

Mr. W. G. Sandford queried if the objection could not be met by leaving out the band. The Clerk said it was possible they might get the engineer to say the Pier was a protection work. Mr. G. Riches, jun., thought it might be so erected as to form one.

As to the band, they ought not to leave that out until they were compelled to. Mr. J. Smith proposed that the preamble of the Bill should exclude power to provide a band. Mr. J. Curtis seconded. Mr. Jarvis moved as an amendment that no alteration should be made.

This was seconded by Mr. Puxley and carried by 6 to 5. The Clerk reported thirty-eight applications had been received for the position of engineer.

To inquiries made of various seaside places as to the persons they had employed in similar work twenty replies had been sent.

The Commissioners then went into the applications, and decided to ask four of the applicants to see them at an early date with a view to a choice being made.

*Norfolk Museums Service, Cromer Museum, CRRMU : 1982.14.19
East shelter under construction – Thursday, 18th August, 1898*

Eastern Evening News: Saturday 27th August 1898

There is to be a new pier at Cromer; but from all that has crept into the public prints it seems as if the townspeople have not yet begun to excite themselves as to what its scale and character shall be. There is a Bill to be promoted, and there are ways and means to be considered. Then, presumably, the question will arise whether the town shall aim simply at replacing the old makeshift which the gale swept away, or whether it shall treat itself to something luxuriously up to date.

Of all the east coast resorts Cromer, probably, is the one least able to dispense with a pier. The old town has no plage, and never can have. Without a landing stage, and a landing stage pre-supposes a pier, it must for ever be cut off from the advantages which follow in the wake of the passenger and excursion steamer. It has all the greater opportunity to distinguish itself, in that on the whole of the Norfolk coast line no pier has yet been erected of first-rate character and dimensions.

The Norfolk Chronicle and Norwich Gazette: Saturday 27th August 1898

The subject and appointment of an engineer for the work contemplated on the sea front was discussed at an adjourned meeting of the Protection Commissioners on Monday. Mr. G. Riches, jun., presided, and there were also present Messrs. J. Curtis, H. Rust, G. Kennedy, W. G. Sandford, A. E. Jarvis, J. Smith, J. Lovelace, T. Puxley, J. Riches, jun., and L. G. Burton.

Four out of the thirty-eight applicants were invited to meet the Board. Of this number all attended, and Mr. W. T. Douglass, M.Inst. C.E., 15, Victoria Street, Westminster, was selected.

On the motion of Mr. Smith, seconded by Mr. Curtis, Mr. Douglass was appointed at a remuneration of five per cent. commission, with a preliminary fee of £100 for preparing the Parliamentary plans to be merged into the work carried out.

Mr. Lovelace had brought forward a motion in favour of appointing an "expert," and named Sir Alexander M. Rendel, of Westminster. The motion, however, was not seconded. It was unanimously decided to erect the new pier on the site of the old jetty.

Eastern Evening News: Thursday 8th September 1898

A meeting of the Board was held yesterday, Mr. G. Riches, jun., in the chair. The minutes of the last meeting, which were confirmed, contained the following resolution – That the works to be included in the Bill about to be promoted are (A) a new pier with pavilion, not exceeding 500 ft. in length, and designed with a view to future extension; (B) the extension of the sea wall as far as the next boundary of the parish; (C) the strengthening and improving of the existing sea wall; (D) the extension of the same eastward; and (E) a new east groyne.

The Clerk reported a debit balance at the bank of £54 5s. 2d. In his statement of work done during the month R. Allen reported that he had pointed 65 yards of sea wall and 40 feet of coping. The eastern sea wall was finished. He had built two sets of brick steps from the promenade to the retaining wall of the east shelter. He had also placed thirty seats in the shelter. The report was adopted, and wage payments by Allen to the amount of £14 9s. 4d., confirmed.

Cheques were ordered to be drawn for the following accounts – Messrs. Barnard, Bishop, & Barnard, seats, &c., £72 3s. 7d.; Cromer Gas and Coke Company, £2 15s. 9d.; Norfolk News Company, advertising, £2 6s.; Messrs. Girling & Smith, erection of shelters, £325 on account; and Messrs. Wrinch & Sons, seats, £27 3s.; total £429 8s. 4d. On the motion of Mr. W. G. Sandford, seconded by Mr. Churchyard, a cheque for £384 7s. 5d., principal and interest on loan was also ordered to be signed.

The Chairman asked what the Board proposed doing now the shelters were finished. He thought some regulations should be made with regard to them.

Also the question of further lighting the East Esplanade should be considered.

Both these matters were then referred to the Works Committee, who will draft regulations as to the shelters and see what extra lighting is wanted on the Board's works.

This concluded the business of the meeting.

The Daily Telegraph: Tuesday 27th September 1898

CROMER

This town is now closing one of the most successful seasons it has ever had.

The loss of the jetty was not an irreparable one, but was probably a blessing in disguise. Father Neptune decided that the front of the town had been disfigured long enough by the unsightly structure, and it has now been decided to apply to Parliament to borrow £50,000 for erecting a pier and to extend the promenades.

During the summer two admirable shelters have been erected on the promenades, and it is to be hoped that next year will see a great many other improvements introduced under the new Act to be obtained from Parliament. A nuisance of which many visitors have complained has been at last abolished on the outskirts of Cromer – pig-keeping.

The Sketch: Wednesday 28th September 1898

Nearly all the seaside resorts have benefited largely this year by the exceptional summer we have had, especially those places which, like Cromer, have recently come into popular favour. I was there six years ago, and again peeped at the place this autumn. What a transformation!

There are now three first-class hotels on the sea-front, the Grand, the Metropole, and the Hotel de Paris, all doing apparently a thriving business, while numerous prosperous-looking red-brick villas have sprung up at the back of the town. Cromer has, however, lost its poor little pier, or "jetty," as it used to be called. The sea washed it away, and it is not, I believe, proposed to build another to take its place.

Eastern Evening News: Thursday 6th October 1898

A general meeting of the Cromer Protection Commissioners was held yesterday at the Clerk's Office, Church Street, Mr. T. Fowell Buxton in the chair. There were present Messrs. R. A. Clarke, J. Riches, J. Bower, J. Lovelace, G. Riches, jun., A. E. Jarvis, H. Rust, G. Kennedy, J. Riches, jun., and L. G. Burton.

A unanimous vote of condolence was passed with the widow and relatives of the late Mr. W. G. Sandford. It was decided that the vacancy on the Board caused by his death should be filled up at the next meeting.

On the recommendation of the Works Committee, it was decided to leave open the west shelter and the lower portion of the east shelter, but to close the upper portion of the latter. Mr. Shanly of London, who wrote asking for permission to place chairs for hire on the Commissioners works, was informed that the Commissioners themselves undertook the provision of seats.

We take the following from the exhaustive report made by Messrs. W. T. Douglass and H. Arnott, the engineers to the Commissioners, addressed to Mr. E. M. Hansell, their Clerk, and considered by the Special Committee: -

15, Victoria Street, Westminster, S.W.,

30th September, 1898.

Cromer Sea Protection Works and Promenade Pier.

SIR – Pursuant to the instructions of your Commissioners, we are submitting for their information a report with plans dealing with the proposed Sea Protection Works and Promenade Pier. We beg to state that we met your committee on the 1st inst. and again on the 8th inst. to consider the general lines which this report should follow. It was thereupon decided that the following work should be dealt with in the first instance, and possible future improvements, included, extending to the eastern and western boundaries of the town.

1. A promenade pier, 500 feet in length and 40 feet in width, designed with a view to future extension, to abut on the Esplanade, opposite the Hotel de Paris, complete with shelters and band stand, pay offices, waiting-rooms, and turnstiles.

2. (A) A sea wall extending from the present termination of the western esplanade to a point opposite the Station Road. (B) The under-pinning of the Western Esplanade wall, and additions of bastions thereto. (C) The construction of a sea wall between the western end of the new East Parade and the Bath Hotel steps, having a level crossing at the gangway, and suitable slip accommodation for the lifeboat and Beach traffic. (D) The extension of the East Parade to the East groyne.

3. (A) The renewal of the eastern groyne. (B) The extension of Doctor's Steps groyne. (C) The reconstruction of Tucker's groyne. (D) The renewal of the shoreward end of the Hotel de Paris groyne.

In addition to the above-mentioned work, the engineers include in their report a plan for the extension of the Western and Eastern Parades as far as the boundary of the parish and the east groyne respectively to be carried out by the Commissioners at a future date if they think fit. In their report the engineers state that the western groynes require to be the shortest, and the eastern groynes the longest. This admits of all shingle which is drawn down and carried over from the western groynes being trapped by those to the east, and in due course washed up by wave action above the high-water mark.

The height of all groynes should be regulated to conform with the Beach level. No groyne should be planked up more than from 12 to 18 inches above the Beach line.

This practice allows the Beach to gather on both sides of the groyne at nearly the same level, a distinct advantage, not only to the groyne itself, but also to the Beach.

The distance apart of groynes on the foreshore should not exceed 180 yards if a uniform Beach is to be maintained.

Indeed a less distance would be advantageous had not the convenience of fishing-boats and bathing machines to be considered. The lengthening of the east groyne about 300 ft., and the Doctor's Steps groyne 180 ft. both to low water mark, will tend in the direction of raising the Beach level between these groynes and the Hotel de Paris groyne.

To assist the functions of the Doctor's Steps groyne in collecting beach under the Bath Hotel and its immediate neighbourhood, a detached low groyne, No. 3 on the plan, will in our opinion be of greater service than the renewal of Tucker's groyne.

The position which this new groyne occupies will scarcely interfere with the bathing machines or shore boats. It will be readily understood that the encroachment on the foreshore is wholly due to the lowering of the Beach towards low water mark.

The raising of the Beach at the foot of the cliff and sea wall will, as a natural result, follow the raising of the lower levels referred to. Hence, this is a point which should be kept constantly in view. It will be advantageous to temporarily lower the western groynes at their shore ends and allow a portion of the Beach to pass on and so raise the foreshore levels in the vicinity of Tucker's groyne.

We are of opinion that all new groynes should be laid down a few points to the westward of a line drawn at right angles to the cliff. The safety of the sea walls will alone be assured by driving back the high-water mark. When the sea breaks heavily against the toe of the sea walls it is propelled upwards, and eventually falls back on to the Beach, which latter it scours out and tends to the undermining of the walls.

We have dealt fully with the foregoing points with a desire to place before your Commissioners the salient features which must always be kept in view when sea defence works are being undertaken. If effect is given to these main points in carrying out a general sea defence scheme at Cromer, we are strongly of opinion that the foreshore levels will be more than maintained and the loss of beach which has been so marked a feature in the past arrested.

Writing with regard to the promenade pier, of which they enclose a design, the engineers state "It is approached from the western esplanade by inclines in front of the Hotel de Paris. Its deck stands 16 ft. above the present Beach level, or on a line with the coping of the esplanade parapet wall.

The pier is 500 ft. in length and 40 ft. in width, with a head 110 ft. wide. The columns are of cast iron, the superstructure of steel and deck of red wood battens, except at the entrance where cast iron perforated plates are substituted. The whole of the work included in this report, and shown on the accompanying plans is of good and substantial construction.

The eastern and western parade walls have an average depth of 12 ft., and the new Esplanade wall 6 ft. below the foundation of the existing wall. The railing provided for the eastern parade is of heavy and ornamental section. For the western parade, where the Beach is fairly high, no railing is provided."

On this report the committee made the following recommendations: -

WEST PARADE EXTENSION: SIZE OF SLIPWAYS. – That the top platform on each slipway should be widened to 30 ft.

WEST PARADE: SIZE OF BASTIONS. – That these should be 40 ft. in diameter, taking the centre from the inside line shown on plan. The committee further recommended that the engineers be instructed to prepare a scheme for reconstructing the slipway adjoining Melbourne House, making the gradient easier, and also for providing accommodation for store room and urinals underneath.

PIER. – The committee recommended that the landing stage should be omitted. The committee recommended that the position of the band stand should be altered so as to leave the centre space between the shelters clearer, and that the same should be constructed so as to be able to be protected from wind from any quarter.

MAIN GANGWAY. – The committee recommended that the engineers should prepare detailed plans and sections for the work shown on the plan as soon as possible, in order that the consent of the Urban District Council might be obtained.

EAST PARADE EXTENSION. – The committee recommended that a slipway be constructed on the further side of the east groyne so as to enable riding horses and carts to pass over the same. It was resolved to recommend that Parliamentary plans be prepared for the full scheme now submitted by the engineers, subject to the foregoing alterations, and the previous settlement of the gangway scheme.

Mr. H. Rust asked if any agreement had been made with the owners of the cliff before the scheme was got out.

The Clerk – No. What land was required would be taken under the Land Clauses Consolidation Act.

Mr. H. Rust thought they did not want to pay for protecting the cliff like they did near the Watch House.

The Clerk – They would have to proceed as did railway companies and other public bodies under the Act he had mentioned.

Mr. H. Rust – But railway companies got land for their own benefit, whereas they would not be doing so, but by their protection work would be increasing the value of the adjoining land.

The Chairman thought it was worth spending money in protection work, but he was certainly against the idea of expending £10,000 on a pier. He thought it would be very hard on the small property holders of the place. The rates were already heavy.

Mr. J. Riches said the work would not require a higher rate than they were now paying.

Mr. G. Riches thought most of the people in Cromer wished to have a pier. To be without one this year had been a great drawback.

The Chairman thought if gentlemen wished to have a pier they should take the risk.

Mr. Burton said Cromer owners and ratepayers liked to manage their own affairs and have a pier in their own hands.

The Chairman – Well, gentlemen, I still differ from you as to the pier.

The report and recommendation of the committee were then put to the meeting and adopted with but one alteration. This had reference to the height of the deck of the pier, which on the motion of Mr. J. Riches, seconded by Mr. H. Rust, it was decided should be raised to 1 ft. 4 in. above the top of the present retaining wall.

It was resolved that R. Allen should be employed to do the necessary work of preparing for the reconstruction of the upper portion of the

Hotel de Paris groyne, to be carried out under the superintendence of the engineers, Messrs. Douglass & Arnott.

Eastern Evening News: Thursday 3rd November 1898

A general meeting of the Board was held yesterday at the Clerk's Office, Church Street, Cromer, Mr. T. Fowell Buxton in the chair.

The Clerk read a letter received from the widow of the late Mr. W. G. Sandford, acknowledging the Board's vote of sympathy passed at the last meeting.

The Special Committee reported that at a meeting held on 12th October the Clerk produced a plan prepared by Messrs. Douglass & Arnott, showing the alteration as proposed by them for the main gangway and crossing from the West to the East Esplanade, and, after discussion, it was agreed to postpone the further consideration until Mr. Douglass could attend before the committee.

The Clerk produced a list of seaside towns sent by Messrs. Douglass & Arnott, with particulars as to the piers, &c., and it was decided that a small committee should visit certain of them. At a meeting held on 18th October Mr. Douglass attended, and discussed with the committee the proposed scheme for the gangway improvement, and, after inspecting the spot and present works, the committee instructed Mr. Douglass to prepare a further plan, which was produced at a meeting held on 26th October, when it was resolved that the same was a practical scheme for the consideration of the two bodies, and that the plan be forwarded at once to the Highways Committee of the Urban District Council.

At a meeting of the Special Committee held 31st October, a letter was received from Messrs. Douglass & Arnott, recommending that the deck of the pier should be on a level with the present retaining wall, and not 1 ft. 4 in. higher, as decided by the Commissioners, but the committee resolved to adhere to the resolution of the Commissioners.

The Clerk produced a plan of the gangway improvement, and a communication received from the Clerk to the Urban District Council, reporting the result of the Highways Committee meeting thereon, was considered, and it was resolved that the conditions suggested by that committee should be recommended to the Commissioners for adoption.

The sub-committee appointed to visit the seaside towns made the following recommendations with reference to the pier and promenade, which were approved by the Special Committee: -

That the kiosks adopted be similar to those at Margate, which have six sides each, and are 9 feet across, or those at Dover that open on one side, and are fitted up inside with seats, and that the roofing be like that of the Ventnor Pavilion, which would be most effective; that the shelters be similar to those on Ventnor Pier, with a few alterations.

Those at Ventnor have glass divisions and roof over top, and one covered with canvas in the form of a tent, which can be removed or erected at any time; also that provision be made for closing ends with revolving shutters, similar to band stand shutters at Margate, or other suitable method; that the flooring of the pier be similar to Ventnor and laid lengthways ¼ in. apart, the portion next retaining wall to be wood lattice work, similar to that at Herne Bay, where the deck at the entrance above high-water mark is laid with cross splines and battens instead of cast iron gratings, so as to offer less resistance to the waves; that the gates be of iron, similar to those at Dover and that the sloping approaches be divided by balustrades, similar to that at Shanklin, but slightly heavier, and turned instead of square; that the sloping approaches and steps between same be paved with material similar to the finer pavement at Southsea, and that provision be made to fix a canvas awning the whole length on either side of the Pier as a shield from the winds when necessary, and that the new promenade be paved in a similar way to the tar paving at Dover, which is very hard and of a fine smooth surface; and that lamps be fixed both sides of the Pier at 15 to 20 yards apart, similar to Ventnor.

The committee express their strong opinion, after visiting these various piers, that the interests of the town would be best served by retaining entire control of the Pier, and not by having it controlled by a public or private company. On being put to the meeting the report and recommendation of the committee were adopted, the Chairman alone dissenting. A cheque was ordered to be drawn for £20 2s. for the expenses of the visiting committee.

The Clerk called attention to the obstruction caused by boats placed on the east promenade. On the motion of Mr. G. Riches, jun., seconded by Mr. J. Lovelace, it was decided to allow the boats to be stored in the recess of the promenade during the winter months, but no repairs to boats or baiting of lines was to be allowed thereon. For the vacancy on the Board caused by the death of Mr. W. G. Sandford, Mr. J. Riches, jun., proposed the election of Mr. Ambrose Burton. Mr. T. Puxley seconded.

Mr. G. Riches, jun., moved, as an amendment, that Mr. Henry A. Barclay should be elected. This Mr. Bower seconded. On a division, Mr. Burton was returned, Mr. Barclay only securing four votes. The meeting was then adjourned to Wednesday, the 23rd.

Eastern Evening News: Thursday 24th November 1898

An adjourned general meeting of the Cromer Protection Commissioners was held yesterday at the Clerk's Office, Church Street. Mr. J. Riches, jun., took the chair, and there were present the Rev. J. F. Sheldon, and Messrs. J. Curtis, F. W. Rogers, R. A. Clarke, L. G. Burton, J. Riches, H. Rust, J. Bower, G. M. Bultitude, A. E. Jarvis, G. Riches, jun., J. Lovelace, T. Puxley and Ambrose Burton.

The last named made the usual declaration on taking his seat for the first time since the election, as successor to the late Mr. W. G. Sandford. A vote of condolence was passed to the relatives of the late Mr. Augustus Mace, a member of the Board at the time of his decease. The vacancy caused will be filled at the next meeting, when Mr. G. Riches, jun., will propose the election of Mr. H. A. Barclay.

The Special Committee reported that, arising out of a letter received from Mr. Sydney Buxton, M.P., on behalf of himself and other owners of property in the town with reference to the dimensions of the proposed pier and the erections to be placed thereon.

Mr. Buxton and Mr. H. A. Barclay attended a meeting of the committee held on Monday, 21st November. After discussion Mr. Buxton stated that he and Mr. Barclay would be willing to abandon their intention of opposing the Bill, as intimated in the letter (but without prejudice to anything subsequently appearing in the Bill when finally drafted) if the Commissioners would undertake:

(1) That a clause should be inserted in the Bill to the effect (a) that no pavilion or refreshment rooms or conveniences be erected, except only a band-stand and shelter and toll office; (b) that no charge except only the toll (which may be varied at the discretion of the local authority) be charged on or in connection with the pier, and that no sale or distribution

of any commodity, except programmes, be allowed thereon; (c) that no dancing saloon be at any future time erected on the pier, and that dancing be prohibited. (2) The omission of clauses in the Bill as drafted having reference to landing stages and tramways on the pier.

The committee considered the proposals made, and recommended the Commissioners to adopt them, and that a clause to that effect be inserted in the Bill.

On the consideration of the report, Mr. Curtis asked who objected to dancing.

The Rev. J. F. Sheldon knew no less than six persons who were down here when there was dancing on the jetty who had not come to Cromer again.

Mr. J. Curtis objected to the action of persons who were able to have dancing in their own houses opposing.

The Rev. J. F. Sheldon said to make the pier a public dancing place would deteriorate the character of the town. [Hear, hear.]

Mr. J. Curtis said his dancing days were over, but he didn't see why they should prevent others from indulging in the exercise.

Mr. F. W. Rogers said when the Special Committee considered the question they had no idea of allowing dancing on the Pier.

Mr. G. Riches, jun., added that the objections raised by Mr. Buxton and others in no way clashed with the opinion of the committee.

Mr. J. Curtis – Why not include other folks as well as that family?

Mr. G. Riches, jun., moved the adoption of the report.

Mr. T. Puxley thought the Board had made a great mistake in electing the Special Committee. It seemed to him they had entirely taken the power out of the hands of the Commissioners. He, for one, thought that a pavilion should be provided, as was the case in other towns.

The Clerk submitted the plan of the pier, which showed no such provision was made.

The Rev. J. F. Sheldon did not think everyone wanted a pavilion.

Mr. T. Puxley felt the time had come when people with enterprise who had speculated in the town wanted some return for their money.

They did not want to be fossilised as in the old days and be restricted in their action by rich people.

Mr. F. W. Rogers said it was always understood there would be no pavilion.

Mr. G. Riches, jun., considered it would be a misfortune to Cromer if they had one. The question was should the committee's report be adopted, or allow a company to come in and ruin the place. If they kept the matter in their own hands they could keep up the tone of the town.

Mr. T. Puxley said he did not want a music hall, but that the place should be such that a concert could be held therein, say for instance in the summer months in aid of the band fund. He therefore moved an amendment to the effect that the band stand should be constructed with the necessary means of sheltering it, and adapted for the holding of concerts.

Mr. A. E. Jarvis seconded the adoption of the report, and pointed out that places like Bournemouth did without a pavilion on their pier exactly as it was proposed to do in this case. There was also a point he thought some Commissioners did not understand. By adopting the report they had Mr. Buxton on their side.

If it was rejected he was afraid he would go forward with his opposition and others with him. And not only that, but some of the guarantors would follow, and the whole Guarantee Fund be upset.

Mr. G. Riches, jun., said much that Mr. Puxley asked for was already provided in the way of shelters.

Mr. A. E. Jarvis said they would never get anyone to go down and sing on the Pier.

The Rev. J. F. Sheldon thought all musical requirements would be amply met by a good band.

Mr. Puxley failed to obtain a seconder for his amendment, and the report of the committee was then adopted.

The Clerk produced the Draft Amended Bill and the old Act, and explained the alterations made.

He was instructed to attend the meeting of the Highways Committee of the Urban District Council with a view of making the like explanatory statement. On Wednesday, 7th December, the final draft of the Bill will be laid before the Commissioners for their inspection and approval.

The Evening Star and Daily Herald: Thursday 1st December 1898

NEXT SESSION'S PRIVATE BILLS
AN INCREASED BUSINESS

On Wednesday night, the period allowed by the Parliamentary Standing Orders expired for the deposit of private Bills and Provisional Orders intended to be promoted next session, and that require to be accompanied by engineering plans and other documents.

At the Private Bills Office there were deposited 363 Bills and Orders, as against 335 last year, an increase of 28.

The local Bills include the Great Eastern Railway Bill, Cromer Protection, Cambridge University and Town Gas, Great Yarmouth Pier, Great Yarmouth Corporation, Great Yarmouth Waterworks Company, Lowestoft Water and Gas Company, South Essex Water Works, Chelmsford Public Recreation Ground ..... and Cromer Electric Lighting P.O.

Eastern Evening News: Thursday 8th December 1898

A general meeting of the Cromer Protection Commissioners was held yesterday at the Clerk's Office, Church Street, Mr. H. Rust in the chair.

The Clerk reported a balance at the bank of £367 15s. 1d., and that during the month rates to the amount of £479 17s. 2d. had been collected.

In presenting R. Allen's report, he stated that the men engaged on the jetty groyne work had gone on strike that morning.

They wanted more money and asked for 3s. 6d. a tide. Allen was called into the room, and in reply to questions, stated the position of affairs. On the motion of Mr. Curtis, seconded by Mr. Clarke, it was decided to give the men the sum asked for.

Wage payments by R. Allen to the amount of £11 6s. 2d. were confirmed.

To fill the vacancy on the Board caused by the death of Mr. A. Mace, Mr. G. Riches, jun., moved and Mr. Churchyard seconded the election of Mr. H. A. Barclay. This was agreed to.

The Special Committee reported that Mr. S. Hoare, M.P., had written under date 28th November, stating that he desired that his name should remain as a guarantor for £35 towards the expenses of the Act, although he had ceased to be a Commissioner.

A letter of the same date had also been received from Mr. Sydney Buxton, M.P. stating that he and Sir Thomas Fowell Buxton, Mr. Richard Hoare, Miss Anna Buxton, Mr. H. A. Barclay, Mr. J. H. Buxton and Mr. Frank Barclay were willing to become guarantors for the sum of £35 each.

The committee recommended that the thanks of the Commissioners be given to Mr. Hoare and Mr. Sydney Buxton for himself and the other guarantors for their offer.

The Clerk had reported to the committee that he had written to Mr. Sydney Buxton as to acceptance of his proposals by the Commissioners, and stated that the Commissioners wished him to understand that there would be nothing inserted in the Act which would prevent concerts being held on the pier, if the Commissioners thought fit, at a future date.

The Clerk had also read Mr. Buxton's reply, dated 25th November, acknowledging this letter. The report, on the motion of Mr. Curtis, seconded by Mr. J. Riches, was adopted.

The Works Committee reported that during the last two months there had been a considerable settlement on the approaches opposite the Hotel de Paris.

They recommended that two concrete buttresses should be placed adjoining the weakest parts, the foundation of the buttresses to be below the foundation of the present promenade.

On the motion of Mr. Churchyard, seconded by Mr. Puxley, the Works Committee were requested to produce at the next meeting a plan of what was proposed to be done.

The Commissioners, on the recommendation of the Special Committee, then adjourned until Wednesday next at 2:30 p.m.

Chapter Three – 1899

The Evening Star and Daily Herald:
Wednesday 11th January 1899

The monthly meeting of the Cromer Urban District Council was held on Monday night, at the offices of the Clerk (Mr. P. E. Hansell). Mr. G. Riches, jun., presiding. – It was decided to adopt the Cameron tank system of sewage-treatment, as experimented upon at Exeter, the same to cost £2,000, sanction to be obtained of the Local Government Board for leave to borrow such sum.

The system is Cameron's, whose firm will supply the necessary tanks, etc., for £420 and which will be calculated for a population of 10,000. The tanks will be situated on the western gangway, immediately beneath residences. – It was further decided to apply to the Local Government Board to sanction a loan of £1,000 for making up and sewering (sic) Cabbell and Cadogan Roads and Jubilee Lane.

It was stated that probable opposition would arise to the Bill about to be promoted in Parliament by the Protection Commissioners, owing to their refusal to erect a pavilion on the proposed pier. – Mr. H. Broadhurst, M.P., spoke strongly against such action, as a concert pavilion would be inimitable to the highest and best interests of the town.

The Norfolk Chronicle and Norwich Gazette:
Saturday 25th February 1899

PARLIAMENTARY

On Monday the Cromer Protection, the Great Yarmouth Corporation, and the Great Yarmouth Pier Bills were read a second time.

Norwich Mercury: Saturday 18th March 1899

A Select Committee of the House of Lords sat on Tuesday to consider the Cromer Protection Bill for the erection of a sea wall and pier at Cromer. Earl Derby presided, and the other members of the committee were Lord

Wimborne, Lord Newton, Earl Stamford, and Lord Sinclair. Mr. Freeman, Q.C., and Mr. Moon appeared for the promoters, and Mr. Hans Hamilton represented the Cabbell trustees, who opposed the Bill.

Mr. Freeman, Q.C., in opening the case for the Bill, explained the circumstances attending the development of Cromer as a health resort, and the depredations and encroachments of the sea, which in 1897 resulted in the sweeping away of the Jetty.

It then became evident that further protective works would be required, and the existing Commissioners, with the approval of the District Council, therefore proposed to extend the sea wall east and west and erect a pleasure pier, at a cost of £45,000.

The petitioners against the Bill were large property owners in the district, and they asked for direct representation upon the new body of Commissioners which was to be constituted under the Bill.

The only alteration proposed in the constitution of the body was to strike out the four ex officio trustees, the rector, the curate, and two church wardens, and to make the remainder directly representative of the ratepayers. At the suggestion of the petitioners the promoters were quite willing to reduce the number of years for the compulsory purchase of the lands from seven to four years, but they could not consent to a reduction of the period of ten years for the execution of works.

The petitioners further stipulated that precedence should be given in the Bill to the works on the west side of the town, which works, they urged, ought to be preceded with first and completed within a limited period, and before the proposed works on the east side were undertaken.

To this counsel replied that he did not think the Commissioners would object to going on with the works on the west side of the town as speedily as practicable; in fact, they would be prepared to take them at once; but they objected to be put under any obligation to proceed with so much of the sea-wall as extended westward to the exclusion of simultaneous attention to the eastern side.

The Commissioners would, no doubt, proceed with that portion of the work which was most urgently required, but they ought to be left free, as the best judges, as to the order in which the different portions of their scheme should be carried out.

The residents and owners on the east side – the more crowded district, were those who would have to bear the main burden of the cost, while those who would reap the chief advantage were the owners of property on the western side.

In conclusion, counsel said he hoped that when their lordships had heard the evidence in support of the Bill they would say that it ought to pass.

Evidence was then called in support of the Bill. At a later stage in the proceedings Mr. Pritchard (Messrs. Sharpe, Parker, Pritchard, and Co., the Parliamentary agents) appeared before the committee, and stated that the promoters had settled terms with the petitioners, and they would bring up amended clauses in accordance with that agreement. The hearing was accordingly adjourned.

The Norfolk Chronicle and Norwich Gazette: Saturday 18th March 1899

A Select Committee of the House of Lords, presided over by Lord Derby, had under consideration, on Tuesday, the Bill promoted by the Cromer Protection Commissioners.

Mr. Freeman, Q.C., who, with Mr. Moon, appeared for the promoters, said Cromer had always suffered from the encroachments of the sea, and from 1845 onwards sums of money had been spent on a sea wall to meet these encroachments.

In 1891 the population had grown to 2,200; it was now estimated at 3,470, which number in the summer months would probably be more than doubled.

The rateable value of the town was £27,195. Four large hotels had been built in the last few years. The extension of the place had made it clear for some time that considerably larger works than those at present existing were needed, and matters were brought to a head in 1897, when the jetty was swept bodily away.

The present Bill proposed to extend the sea-wall along the remainder of the front, both east and west, and to construct a pier 183 yards long, to be used solely for pleasure purposes, the estimated cost being £45,000. Mr. Hansell, the clerk to the Protection Commission, gave evidence, and the Bill will be further considered at the next meeting of the committee.

On Thursday, the Parliamentary Agent brought up the clauses which had been arranged to carry out the compromise agreed upon. The committee approved the clauses and passed the Bill, ordering it to be reported for third reading.

The Norwich Mercury: Saturday 25th March 1899

CROMER PROTECTION BILL

This Bill, which is promoted by the Cromer Protection Commissioners, has for its object, as already described, the construction of a sea wall and pier, was again brought before the Select Committee of the House of Lords on Thursday in last week.

The preamble had already been passed, but certain clauses remained for settlement, and these were now considered. Mr. Pritchard (of Messrs. Sharpe, Parker, Pritchard, and Co., Parliamentary agents) conducted the case for the promoters, and produced copies of the amended clauses.

The alterations related mainly to details. One of some importance was designed to give effect to the desire of the petitioning Cabbell Trustees, of the Cromer Hall Estate, as to proceeding with that portion of the proposed works on the western side of the town sea-front as speedily as possible; and another modification, introduced in the interest of the same trustees and other land owners, gave them a right of pre-emption in the event of any surplus land acquired by the Commissioners under the present Bill being hereafter sold.

These amendments, having been made in the several clauses to which they referred, the Bill was ordered to be reported to the House. The proceedings then terminated.

The Norfolk News (Second Sheet): Saturday 15th April 1899

In the Commons on Tuesday the Cromer Protection Bill was read a second time, and committed. It has already been through the Upper House.

Sunday Daily Telegraph: Sunday 7th May 1899

CROMER

Everything points to a continuance of the present brilliant weather. The scenery of the district is now at its grandest.

No music will be obtainable on Sundays this year, as bands have now to rely on voluntary subscriptions, and sufficient funds will not be available for the purpose.

Next year bands and amusements will be provided out of the rates, and a venture in the direction indicated may be made.

Down trains: Liverpool Street, 9.50 a.m.; 3.30 p.m.
Up trains: 1.00 p.m., 4.50, 7.50.

The Walsall Advertiser: Saturday 27th May 1899

Cromer was reached at ten o' clock. We were unable to get accommodated only at a temperance hotel, which, although of a good class, is not much to the liking of our members. Cromer is a most disappointing place. There is no pier or any other attractions whatever. It stands high and bracing on its breezy cliffs overlooking the North Sea. Its church is a prominent landmark. The cliffs are of sand, and wild flowers grow in great variety on their summits. It is fortified by an esplanade and breakwater, its exposed position being plainly shewn by the new lighthouse.

The Norfolk Chronicle and Norwich Gazette:
Saturday 10th June 1899

CROMER.

PROTECTION FROM THE SEA.

NOTICE is Hereby Given, that Commissioners acting in the execution of the Act, intituled "An Act to authorise the Erection of Sea Walls and Works, and a Jetty at the Town or Parish of Cromer, in the County of Norfolk, and otherwise to provide for protecting the said Town and Parish from the further Encroachment of the Sea," intend to hold a MEETING at the Clerk's Office in Cromer aforesaid, on Wednesday, the 21st day of June inst., at Half-past Two o'clock in the Afternoon, for the purpose of making a Rate under the authority of the said Act; and that a statement of the Rate will be deposited at the Clerk's Office aforesaid, for Inspection on and after the 14th day of June inst.

P. E. HANSELL,
Clerk to the Commissioners.
Church Street, Cromer, 7th June, 1899.   956

NOTICE.

EXTENSION OF GROYNES AT CROMER.

NOTICE is Hereby Given, that an application has been received by the Board of Trade (to whom by the Crown Lands Act, 1866, the management of the rights and interests of the Crown in the Foreshores of the United Kingdom has been transferred) from the Cromer Protection Commissioners for permission to extend seaward the two existing Groynes on the Eastern side of the Coast Guard Station at Cromer.

The Eastern Groyne will be extended 300 feet and the Western Groyne 200 feet.

All persons interested are to take Notice that, 21 days after this date, the Board of Trade will proceed to consider the application, and, in the meantime, they will receive any objections which may be made thereto.

T. H. W. PELHAM,
Assistant Secretary.

Board of Trade,
Harbour Department,
9th day of June, 1899.   955

The Norwich Mercury: Saturday 10th June 1899

A general meeting of the Board was held on Wednesday at the Clerk's Office, Church Street, Mr. F. W. Rogers in the chair.

The Works Committee recommended that the Doctor's Steps breakwater should be extended 200 feet and the East breakwater 300 feet, and the necessary plans be prepared by Mr. Douglass, the engineer. This was agreed to, and it was also decided to take the required steps to obtain the permission of the Board of Trade to the extension.

On the recommendation of the same committee, it was resolved to close the east shelter at 10 o'clock each night; also to put up warning notices in both shelters against persons improperly using or doing damage to them.

It was further decided to have the ironwork portions of the shelter repainted, and to purchase from Mr. Leggett five lamps with double burners at an inclusive cost of £4 2s. each, or £20 10s. in all, for use on the Esplanade.

A cheque for £179 13s. 10d. was directed to be drawn in favour of Messrs. Jewson for timber supplied. Messrs. Douglass and Arnott have written that all matters in dispute had been amicably settled. Messrs. Jewson agreeing to deductions at £14 8s. 4d. and £3, £17 8s. 4d. in all.

It was agreed on the motion of Mr. A. Jarvis, seconded by Mr. J. Lovelace, that R. Balls, "Jetty Keeper," should be paid his increased wages as last year, viz., 22s. per week from 15th June to 1st July, and 32s. per week from that date to the 3rd November.

The Special Committee reported that having been advised by Mr. Douglass that there was no objection, permission had been given for the septic tank system of sewage disposal to be introduced at Cromer by the Urban District Council, to place certain tanks in connection with the scheme on the side of the proposed western promenade. The same committee had considered the question of the preparation of plans, and the commencement of certain works as soon as possible in the event of the Protection Bill passing through Parliament. They recommended that on the Bill receiving the Royal Assent Mr. Douglass should at once prepare plans and specifications: – (1) for the Pier, (2) the Western Parade for a distance of 1,700 feet from the westward of the present Western Parade, (3) the proposed works between the west end of the

East Promenade and the west end of the West Parade, including the underpinning of the wall, (4) the proposed store house and new gangway to the west of Melbourne House, and that the plans for same already prepared be approved.

Mr. Jarvis drew attention to some details on the plan for the Pier which he had not before seen.

The report was ultimately adopted, it being agreed that Mr. Douglass should not proceed with the details of the plan at the entrance to the Pier.

The Works Committee were elected as under: – Messrs. G. Riches, jun., F. W. Rogers, A. E. Jarvis, J. Lovelace, W. Churchyard, J. Bower, and H. Rust. The following were elected the Finance Committee: – Messrs. J. Bower, G. Riches, jun., A. E. Jarvis, H. Rust, and J. Riches, jun., were elected without a division.

On the motion of Mr. W. Churchyard, seconded by Mr. G. Riches, jun., an application by the Band Committee for permission to use the works of the Commissioners during the season was granted.

On the motion of Mr. J. Riches, jun., seconded by Mr. H. Rust, it was decided to hold a special meeting for the purpose of fixing the rate on Wednesday, 21st June.

The Clerk reported that since the last meeting two clauses had been added to the Protection Bill. The first was with regard to the Pier coming within the district of Cromer.

The position of affairs was that the boundary of the parish extended to low water mark, as did also the jurisdiction of the Court. So no offence committed on that part of the Pier could be tried summarily. With the addition of this clause, however, below high-water mark would for all purposes be deemed to be situate in the parish and urban district of Cromer. The second clause gave to the Urban District Council the superintendence of operations at places where the work of the two bodies joined.

The meeting of the Board was adjourned to Wednesday, 21st June.

Eastern Daily Press: Thursday 22nd June 1899

A special and adjourned meeting of the Cromer Protection Commissioners was held yesterday, at the Clerk's Office, Church Street, Mr. F. W. Rogers in the chair. The other members present were Messrs. J. Lovelace, G. Kennedy, G. Riches, jun., and J. Bower.

The business of the meeting was to make a rate for the coming year. In reply to Mr. Lovelace, the Clerk said that for the last four years the rate had been 1s. 6d. in the £, and in recommending a similar amount for the ensuing year gave the following estimate of expenditure; – (1) Present debit at bank £30 12s. 1d., less arrears of rate £18 19s. 2d., balance £11 12s. 11d.; (2) one year's interest and repayment of principle on balance of loan of £700, £392 and interest on overdrawn account £5, total £387; (3) salaries, Clerk £40, Collector £20, Jetty Keeper £45, total £105; (4) ordinary repairs and maintenance of works, including Allen's wages, £100, lighting approaches and Esplanade £25, total £125; (5) sundries, incidental expenses £20; and (6) outstanding accounts and works authorised; engineers' commission on Jetty groyne, £16; new lamps for bandstand, £20; projected extension of Doctor's Steps and east groynes, £700; interest and repayment of principle on new works, £500; total £1,236 12s. 11d.; and total estimated expenditure, £1,894 12s. 11d. A 1s. 6d. rate would raise this sum and leave a balance of £18.

Mr. Lovelace asked if the £18 19s. 2d. mentioned represented all the recoverable arrears. The Clerk – Yes, and that they were sure to obtain. Mr. Lovelace thought the result very satisfactory. They did not often come out as close as that. Mr. G. Riches, jun., thought it very desirable they should get on with the extension of the Doctor's Steps breakwater.

Were that done it would save money in doing works in front of the town, especially at the foot of the gangway. They wanted a quantity of beach such as they would then get there. If they were tied down to a certain limit with regard to the length of the gangway they needed to bring the beach up to meet it. The Clerk said they would not at present proceed further in the matter of the groyne until they heard from the Board of Trade. On the motion of Mr. G. Riches, jun., seconded by Mr. Kennedy, a rate of 1s. 6d. in the £ for the coming year was agreed to.

The Clerk said there appeared to be rather a misunderstanding as to the application made at the last meeting for an overdraft. The reason for that application was not that enough money was not received for last year's estimate.

On the contrary, not only had they carried out the shelters and works included in the estimate of £1,500, but an additional £300 had come in which had been spent on the Jetty groyne. At the present time they had only a debit balance of £11 odd. Mr. G. Riches thought this very satisfactory, and the other members concurred.

The Sheffield and Rotherham Independent: Saturday 24th June 1899

CROMER

The season is one of great promise, and visitors will be more liberally catered for this year than ever was the case. A splendid band has been secured. Orchestral concerts are being provided, and theatrical parties have been engaged for the Town Hall. The Commissioners are making preparations to commence the improvement works on the sea front. Before next season the pier will probably be erected.

Eastern Daily Press: Thursday 6th July 1899

A general meeting of the Protection Commissioners was held yesterday at the Clerk's Office, Church Street, Mr. G. Riches, jun., presided.

Wage payments by R. Allen to the amount of £8 2s. were confirmed.

A cheque for £8 9s. for wages for R. Balls, Jetty Keeper, was ordered to be signed.

On the motion of Mr. J. Bower, seconded by Mr. F. W. Rogers, it was decided he be paid monthly in the future.

The question of the extension of the groynes was referred to the Works Committee to consult with the engineer on the subject.

The East London Advertiser: Saturday 15th July 1899

Cromer is a favourite watering-place on the prettiest part of the Norfolk coast, 24 miles from Norwich. Few places combine in a greater degree the advantages of a salubrious and invigorating air with a fine and open sea and beautiful scenery.

There are several good hotels, and many well-furnished lodging houses for the accommodation of visitors. There is now a golf club, with splendid links (18 holes), at Cromer.

The roads are admirable for cycling. The express trains from Liverpool St. do the journey in two hours and fifty-five minutes, being run through with only one stop.

Restaurant cars are run. There is no pier at Cromer.

The Daily Telegraph: Friday 28th July 1899

Cromer – Visitors are enjoying charming weather. Rain descended heavily last Sunday, and the country is now looking much fresher. The season is proving better than had been anticipated, the loss of the jetty being keenly felt, and with improved band arrangements, and a capital bill of fare at the Town Hall it is anticipated that August will be quite up to the average.

Boating is much indulged in, and golfing is now at its height. Prosecutions have taken place on account of the regulations not being observed in respect to mixed bathing.

Hotels. –   Grand and Metropole, facing sea.
"   Royal Links, adjoining 18 Hole Golf Links.

Eastern Daily Press: Thursday 3rd August 1899

A general meeting was held yesterday at the Clerk's Office, Church Street, Cromer.

There were present Messrs. G. Riches, jun., (Chairman), H. Rust, G. Kennedy, Ambrose Burton, J. Jillings, H. A. Barclay, J. Riches, jun., L. G. Burton, R. A. Clarke, A. E. Jarvis, T. Puxley, and J. Lovelace.

The Clerk reported a credit balance at the bank of £290 4s. 1½d., also since last report rates to the amount of £325 11s. 6d. had been collected. On the motion of Mr. Clarke, seconded by Mr. Barclay, wage payments by R. Allen to the extent of £8 were confirmed.

The Works Committee reported that Mr. Douglass, the engineer, had attended their meeting on the 19th July, and produced plans of the works proposed to be carried out in the first instance on the passing of the Bill.

After discussing the plans and giving certain instructions to Mr. Douglass as to the approaches to the Pier, the engineer was requested to complete the plans as soon as possible and to attend an adjourned meeting of the August general meeting.

Mr. Douglass was also instructed to consider the possibility of constructing a portion of the Pier so as to be ready for use next season and to report thereon at the next meeting. The report was adopted on the motion of Mr. Barclay, seconded by Mr. Jarvis.

The Clerk read a letter from Miss Cooper asking permission to make collections on the Commissioners' Works between the hours of 9 and 7 on Hospital Saturday, August 19th. Mr. Barclay proposed, Mr. Clarke seconded, and it was agreed to inform the applicant that there would be no objection to the course suggested.

An application was received through Mr. W. Moulton for leave of the Commissioners being given to the band of the Port of Hull Societies' Orphan Home performing on the East and West Esplanade on Friday, 18th August. The Chairman expressed his opinion that this band should not clash with the season band, and Mr. Jarvis suggested that from 1.30 to 3 would be a suitable time.

Mr. Kennedy said a collection between those hours would not be sufficient. As the boys were only here for a very short time he would give them a chance. He thought that for the day they might do away with the other band. On the motion of Mr. Puxley, seconded by Mr. Kennedy, the matter was referred to the committee.

The Clerk reported that the Protection Bill passed the House of Commons in the form in which the Commissioners had last seen it. It now only awaited the Royal Assent to become law.

The Chairman thought this very satisfactory. Mr. Douglass, the engineer, wrote suggesting Thursday August 10th, for meeting the Board, with regard to the plans, &c., of the new work, and it was decided that the meeting should be held at 2.30 p.m. that day.

The Chairman called attention to the great need existing for additional seating accommodation on the Esplanade. As in all probability the Board would require a great number of seats for the Pier, he thought they might get some now for the use of visitors.

He favoured reversible back seats similar to those he had seen at Torquay. He thought the Board might give their sanction to an outlay of £20 or £30 in this direction.

Mr. Jarvis also emphasised the need for more seats. Mr. Puxley thought they should have some at once, and proposed that the Works Committee should be authorised to purchase one hundred seats and place them on the Esplanade. Mr. Jarvis seconded. Mr. J. Lovelace moved as an amendment that only sixty be purchased.

Mr. J. Riches, jun., seconded. On a division there was five for and five against the amendment, and by the casting vote of the Chairman Mr. Puxley's motion was carried. The meeting was then adjourned to Thursday next at 2.30 p.m.

Norfolk Museums Service, Cromer Museum, CRRMU :
1981.80.1471.193
Cromer's west promenade

The Daily Telegraph: Friday 4th August 1899

CROMER

A clouded sky yesterday was almost a welcome change, succeeding as it did a number of extremely hot days. The weather has, indeed, been superb, and its effect is marked in the great increase of visitors now in the town.

The Commissioners are hopeful that a portion of the new pier about to be erected will be available for public use next year. The bastion of the old jetty is crowded each day while the band of the Gloucester Hussars performs.

The annual regatta is fixed for the 17th inst. Drives for the purpose of viewing the beautiful scenery of the district are the chief attraction, but bathing, boating, and golfing have their share of followers.

Norfolk Museums Service, Cromer Museum, CRRMU : 1979.72.49
The Hotel de Paris, east beach, showing the old jetty bastion

Cromer Protection Act 1899

"The Commissioners may notwithstanding any public rights of way and other rights make and maintain in the lines and according to the levels shown on the deposited plans and sections the works following (that is to say): –

A sea wall or embankment and promenade (in this Act called "the promenade") in the parish of Cromer;

A pier (in this Act called "the pier") commencing on the promenade in front of the Hotel de Paris in the parish of Cromer and extending thence for a distance of 183 yards in a northerly direction".

"If the works authorised by this Act and shown on the deposited plans are not completed within ten years from the passing of this Act then on the expiration of that period the powers by this Act granted to the Commissioners for the making thereof or otherwise in relation thereto shall cease except as to so much thereof as shall then be completed Provided that the Commissioners may construct such improvements and extensions of and additions to the works constructed under the powers of this Act as may from time to time be necessary for the protection of the parish of Cromer".

"The Commissioners may construct provide work and use all proper landing-stages landing-places lamps lamp-posts roads footpaths sheds toll-houses toll-gates or bars cranes lifts weighing-machines buoys moorings sewers drains and other works and conveniences connected with the works (other than the pier) by this Act authorised or under the control of the Commissioners".

"The Commissioners may erect and construct upon the pier or within the limits of deviation of the pier as shown on the deposited plans bandstands shelters seats toll-houses toll-gates or bars lamps and lamp-posts but no other erection whatever and may make such charges for the use thereof or for admission thereto as they may think fit and they may furnish and equip the same".

"The Commissioners may dredge scour and deepen the bed and shore of the sea at or near to any part of the pier".

THE CONSTRUCTION OF CROMER PIER

"The pier shall not be used except for the purpose of recreation including musical performances Provided that dancing shall not be allowed to take place thereon and that no sale or distribution of any commodity (except programmes) be allowed thereon".

"The Commissioners may demand recover and receive for the use of the pier any sums not exceeding the rates specified in the Forth Schedule to this Act".

"The Commissioners may grant to promenaders or others pass or family tickets for the use of the pier on such terms and for such periods not exceeding one year as may be agreed but so that no preference be given to any person A pass or family ticket shall not be transferable and shall not be used except by the person or by members of the family to whom or for whose use it is granted If any person wilfully and with intent to defraud act in any way in contravention of this provision or use or attempt to use any false or counterfeit or expired ticket he shall for every such offence be liable to a penalty not exceeding twenty shillings".

"The Commissioners may on any occasion which they may deem special but not on more than twelve days in any one year nor more than three days in succession close their pier against the public and may on such occasions charge such special rates of admission not exceeding one shilling for each person as the Commissioners may think fit".

"Officers of police being in the execution of their duty shall at all times have free ingress passage and egress to or along and from the pier by land without payment".

"All persons using any apparatus for saving life and being persons either belonging to the coastguard or being persons for the time being actually employed in saving life or in exercising or using the apparatus for saving life and also all persons brought ashore from any vessel in distress by means of such apparatus shall at all times have free ingress passage and egress to along and from the pier without payment".

"The officers of the coastguard and all other persons for the time being actually employed in connection with the apparatus for saving life may either permanently or temporarily without payment attach or cause to be attached to any part of the pier spars and other apparatus for saving life and may also either in course of using or of exercising the apparatus for saving life fire rockets over the pier".

"The Commissioners shall at all times keep at the outer extremity of the pier a sufficient number of efficient life-buoys and lines in good order and fit and ready for use".

"The Commissioners may lease for any term not exceeding seven years the rates and other charges authorised to be taken in respect of their pier and may let for hire or lease for any term not exceeding seven years any band-stands and other erections to any person upon such terms and conditions as they think fit and the lessee of the said rates and charges during the continuance of his lease and to the extent provided in such lease shall have and may exercise all or any of the powers conferred upon the Commissioners by this Act of levying and recovering rates and charges and shall be subject to the same provisions in respect thereto as the Commissioners are under this Act".

"If a work constructed by the Commissioners on in over through or across tidal lands or a tidal water is abandoned or suffered to fall into decay the Board of Trade may abate and remove the work or any part of it and restore the site thereof to its former condition at the expense of the Commissioners and the amount of such expense shall be a debt due from the Commissioners to the Crown and shall be recoverable as a Crown debt or summarily".

"The Commissioners shall at or near to the works below high-water mark authorised by this Act during the whole time of the constructing altering or extending the same exhibit and keep burning at their own expense every night from sunset to sunrise such lights (if any) as the Board of Trade require or approve and if the Commissioners fail to comply in any respect with the provisions of this section they shall for each night in which they so fail be liable to a penalty not exceeding twenty pounds".

"The Commissioners shall at the outer extremity of their works below high-water exhibit and keep burning from sunset to sunrise such lights (if any) as the Corporation of Trinity House shall direct and if the Commissioners fail to comply in any respect with the provisions of this section they shall for each night in which they so fail be liable to a penalty not exceeding twenty pounds".

"In case of injury to or destruction or decay of the pier or works or any part thereof the Commissioners shall lay down such buoys exhibit such lights or take such other means for preventing so far as may be danger to navigation as shall from time to time be directed by the Corporation of Trinity House and shall apply to that corporation for directions as to the means to be taken and the Commissioners shall be liable to a penalty not exceeding ten pounds for every month during which they omit so to apply or refuse or neglect to obey any direction given in reference to the means to be taken".

Forth Schedule – Rates for Use of Pier.

For every person who shall use the pier for the purpose of walking for exercise pleasure or any other purpose.

For each and every time any sum not exceeding ......
6d.

For every bath chair (including the driver) taken on the pier.

For each and every time any sum not exceeding ......
8d.

For every perambulator (including the person in charge).

For each and every time any sum not exceeding ......
6d.

(9th August 1899)

Chapter Three – 1899 (continued)

East Anglian Daily Times: Saturday 12th August 1899

CROMER'S PIER FOR 1900

An adjourned meeting of the Cromer Protection Commissioners was held on Thursday, Mr. A. E. Jarvis presiding. It having been reported that the Royal Assent had been given to the Protection Act promoted by the Commissioners, it was decided that the Clerk should take advice from some financial authority as to the best means of borrowing the necessary sum required to carry out the improvements on the sea front – whether on the security of the Commissioners' own rates, or through the Urban District Council.

The Works Committee reported having met the engineer's assistant, who had produced detailed plans of the improved promenades and the proposed pier.

They recommended that the entrance gates and kiosks be placed at the immediate entrance to the pier proper, and that the accessories be obtained as required, the sub-structure to be carried out by one contractor; that glazed partitions be provided between the sections of the seats, and that the pavement of the approach slopes at the entrance of the pier be of artificial stone.

The Committee went on to recommend that one price be given for the pier sub-structure, and extra price (if any) for stopping at the end of the first wide portion, and second extra price (if any) for stopping at the entrance to the pier head.

Whatever portion was decided upon was to be carried out by June 30th, 1900, and building operations were to be suspended during the summer months. The recommendations of the Committee were unanimously adopted.

Eastern Evening News: Thursday 24th August 1899

An adjourned meeting was held yesterday at the Clerk's Office, Church Street, Cromer, Mr. J. Smith in the chair. There were present Messrs. J. Curtis, R. A. Clarke, H. Rust, A. E. Jarvis, J. Lovelace, G. Riches, jun.,

L. G. Burton, T. Puxley, J. Riches, jun., and Ambrose Burton; Messrs. Douglass and Arnott, the engineers, also attended.

The Works Committee recommended that fourteen plans and two specifications submitted, relative to proposed works, should be approved, subject to the following alterations: – (1) That the parapet wall of the gangway should not extend to the east of the line of the highway to the Beach, (2) that tar paving should not be included in the contracts for sea wall and promenade; (3) that steps should be provided to the Beach opposite the public conveniences, (4) that there should be specifications prepared for pier proper without shelters, &c., (5) that cast-iron be substituted for steel piles, and (6) that the engineers prepare specifications for lighting the whole front and report.

On the motion of Mr. Jarvis, seconded by Mr. R. A. Clarke, the report was adopted, and a further resolution was passed on the motion of Mr. Curtis, seconded by Mr. J. Riches, jun., instructing the engineers to prepare a plan for the further widening of the promenade between the steps opposite the Bath Hotel and those in front of Victoria House.

Arising out of the discussion of these details, Mr. Douglass, in reply to the Chairman, stated that in the construction of the pier they would go 15 ft. below the present surface of the beach. Also that the deck of the pier would be 18 ft. above ordinary high tide.

The Morning Leader (London): Friday 25th August 1899

Cromer – The town is full of visitors, and excursions and picnics to pleasant spots in the district are very popular. Bathing machine and boat owners are also well patronised. The Royal Cromer Golf Club meeting this week was largely attended.

On Monday a foursome competition commences on the same links.

The Countess of Yarborough opened a grand bazaar at Overstrand. Lady Battersea was one of the stall-holders. The Cromer Season Band committee had a garden fête in the grounds of Cliff House, the marine residence of Mr. Arnold F. Hills. Good programs (sic) continue to be provided at the Town Hall entertainments. It is anticipated that a considerable portion of a new pier will be ready for use by next season.

Norfolk Museums Service, Cromer Museum, CRRMU :
1981.80.1471.194
Cromer's east promenade

Eastern Evening News: Thursday 7th September 1899

A general meeting was held yesterday at the Clerk's Office, Church Street, Cromer. Mr. A. E. Jarvis was in the chair, and there were present Messrs. J. Curtis, Ambrose Burton, H. Rust, J. Lovelace, G. Riches, jun., W. Churchyard, G. Kennedy, J. Bower, F. W. Rogers, H. A. Barclay, L. G. Burton, and J. Riches, jun. Messrs. Douglass & Arnott, the engineers, also attended the meeting.

The Clerk reported a credit balance at the bank of £755 13s. 2d. Wage payments by R. Allen to the amount of £10 were confirmed.

The Works Committee made certain recommendations as to details in the erection of the pier.

One was that wrought iron piles should be substituted for the cast iron previously decided upon, and another that one contract should be made for the whole substructure of the pier to be completed by the end of June.

These were agreed to, as were also the engineer's plans for the widening of the promenade between Victoria Boarding-House and the Bath Hotel. The present width opposite the Victoria slope is 17 ft.; under the plan it will be 29 ft.

Also, a slope and return slope approach to the Beach will take the place of the steps opposite the Bath Hotel.

The plans showing alterations to the gangway scheme were also approved. On the recommendation of the same committee, the Clerk and engineers were instructed to settle as to advertising for and the general conditions of contract, and that the committee should open tenders before the next Board meeting, and report to the Commissioners thereon.

It was also decided that all works exclusive of the pier should be divided into two contracts, the west end of the pier approach to mark the dividing line of the two, and that all the works to the east of the Grand Hotel groyne should be completed by the end of June.

The Clerk was also authorised to give notices to treat to the parties concerned for the whole of the Beach and the land on the front required to be taken from the west end of the present promenade for the purpose of this work.

It was decided to hire Mr. Upcher's pile driver, with power to the committee to purchase it at a reasonable price.

The Finance Committee reported with regard to inquiries as to loans that the Urban District Council had been written to and a letter received from the Deputy Clerk stating that the Council was in communication with the Local Government Board on the subject, but up to the present had received no answer from the Department.

The committee also reported that an offer of a loan of £30,000 at 3 ½ per cent. for twelve months had been received from Messrs. Barclay, Limited.

They recommended an acknowledgement of the offer, but the postponement of a decision, the Clerk meanwhile to continue his inquiries.

On the motion of Mr. Rogers, seconded by Mr. Riches, jun., the committee's report was adopted. Mr. H. A. Barclay called attention to the slope at the cliff end of the east groyne. He suggested such an alteration as would make it safe and easy for horses to use it, and offered to contribute towards the cost. The matter was referred to the Works Committee to consider and report.

Eastern Evening News: Thursday 12th October 1899

An adjourned meeting was held yesterday at the Clerk's Office, Church Street, Cromer, Mr. G. Riches, jun., in the chair. There were present Messrs. J. Curtis, J. Lovelace, H. Rust, W. Churchyard, G. Kennedy, J. Smith, H. A. Barclay, T. F. Buxton, L. G. Burton, J. Riches, jun., and G. W. Bultitude.

The Works Committee recommended that the Clerk should be instructed to proceed with Messrs. Anthony Fasey & Son (Leytonstone, London) contract (£8,167 12s. 1d.) for the eastern section, and Messrs. B. Cooke & Co.'s (16, Victoria Street, Westminster) contract (£11,955) for the western section of the new works.

Also, when the consent of the Board of Trade is received, proceed with Mr. Alfred Thorne's (7, Carteret Street, Queen Anne's Gate, Westminster) contract (£11,275) for the pier.

The committee further recommended that the guarantees of the sureties for the west section and the pier works should be £1,000, and for the east works £800. Mr. Curtis proposed the adoption of the report. Mr. Lovelace seconded.

This was agreed to, after the Clerk had informed Mr. J. Riches, jun., that under the conditions of the pier contract one part of the work was to be done by June 30th, 1900, and the remainder by May 31st, 1901.

The Works Committee recommended the appointment of a superintendent of the works at a certain sum per week. Mr. Douglass, the engineer, wrote suggesting Mr. Woodford Pilkington at £4 4s. per week, and the appointment of an assistant at £2 a week. The Chairman supported the recommendation. He said with £30,000 work to be done, extending over a mile in length, it was too much for one man to attend to. Mr. J. Riches, jun., thought a smaller sum might be paid. Mr. T. Fowell

Buxton considered it was good economy to have the work well inspected. [Hear, hear.]

Mr. Rust and Mr. Curtis were also of the same opinion. On the motion of Mr. Buxton, seconded by Mr. Smith, the appointment of Mr. Pilkington was agreed to and the suggestion as to an assistant approved. The Chairman presented a report as to the pile engine, and on the motion of Mr. Curtis, seconded by Mr. Burton, it was resolved to offer Mr. H. M. Upcher £30 for the same. On the suggestion of the Clerk, the meeting was adjourned to Wednesday at 2:30 p.m.

Eastern Evening News: Thursday 19th October 1899

An adjourned meeting was held yesterday at the Clerk's Office, Church Street, Cromer, Mr. G. Riches, jun., in the chair. There were present Messrs. J. Curtis, J. Riches, H. Rust, G. Kennedy, W. Churchyard, F. W. Rogers, J. Smith, T. Puxley, T. F. Buxton, and J. Riches, jun.

The sureties named by Messrs. Cooke & Co. and Messrs. Fasey & Son with reference to their contracts were approved.

An application from Messrs. Cooke & Co. for the use of the west shelter as an office was refused.

A letter was received from the Board of Trade, giving formal consent to the Commissioners borrowing an additional £4,000 for the pier construction over the £11,000 allowed them in the Act.

The whole £15,000 is repayable within a period of sixty years. The extra cost of the pier is due to the rise in the price of iron. In reply to questions as to commencing the pier the Clerk said they could not possibly begin until they had the consent of the Board of Trade.

The Chairman thought that in the meantime they might get on with the approach.

The Clerk read a letter from Messrs. Douglass & Arnott, the engineers, with regard to the west and east contract. This was to the effect that the contractors would be having materials delivered this week, when their agents would also be down, as they were anxious to take advantage of the fine weather.

The Clerk read a letter from Mr. J. Jillings resigning his seat on the Board. A second letter from the same individual contained an application for the position of inspector of the new works. As the filling of this appointment has not yet been considered by the Board, on the motion of Mr. Smith, seconded by Mr. Buxton, it was decided to advertise for applicants.

Mr. Smith proposed, and Mr. Buxton seconded, the payments of bills to the amount of £36 15s. The action of the Clerk in insuring the men at work on the groyne in the Protection Insurance Corporation was approved.

Eastern Daily Press: Monday 23rd October 1899

> SUB-INSPECTOR OF WORKS WANTED
> FOR SEA DEFENCE WORKS and PIER at Cromer; Salary £2 per Week.—Applications to be made to Douglas & Arnott, Engineers, 15, Victoria Street, Westminster, London.

Eastern Evening News: Thursday 2nd November 1899

A general meeting was held yesterday at the Clerk's Office, Church Street, Cromer. Mr. A. E. Jarvis was in the chair, and there were present Messrs. J. Curtis, R. A. Clarke, J. Riches, H. Rust, W. Churchyard, J. Bower, G. Kennedy, A. Burton, J. Riches, jun., L. G. Burton, J. Lovelace, T. Puxley, and G. Riches, jun.

The Clerk reported a credit balance at the bank of £678 13s. 6d. Also that since last statement £209 9s. 6d. had been collected in rates. R. Allen's wage payments, to the amount of £34 11s. 8d., were confirmed. His report as to work on the groynes was also adopted.

On the motion of Mr. Clarke, seconded by Mr. J. Riches, the following payments were authorised: – R. Balls, salary, four weeks, 22s., and allowance for beach for same period, £2; Cromer Gas Co., gas supplied quarter ending Sept. 30th, £3 4s. 3d.; Messrs. English Bros., timber supplied, £84 17s. 1d.; and Messrs. Wade & Co., spikes, &c., £21 6s. 3d. It was decided that R. Balls's salary and allowance for shelters during the winter should be 8s. a week inclusive.

Messrs. Douglass & Arnott, the engineers, reported that Mr. Woodford Pilkington, superintendent of the works, entered on his duties on 23rd inst.

With regard to the eastern section, they stated that Messrs. Fasey & Son, the contractors, were engaged in delivering materials to Cromer, and had thirteen men employed on the work.

The Pier and Bath Hotel bastions and a portion of the sea wall had been set out preliminary to excavating for the foundation of these walls. For the western section of the work Messrs. B. Cooke & Co., the contractors, were this week sending materials and plant to Cromer; and for the third section – that of the Pier – the contractor, Mr. A. Thorne, was making arrangements to get on with the work.

The Works Committee reported that Messrs. Douglass & Arnott attended their meeting that day and produced applications they had received for the post of sub-inspector. They recommended that Mr. J. H. Lowe of Weymouth be appointed at a salary of £2 per week.

The Clerk having reported that the time given in the notices to treat (with regard to land required by the Commissioners) had nearly expired, it was recommended that the committee be empowered to treat with the owners as to the necessary purchases, but not to settle, and that they report in due course to the Board.

The Clerk read the list of applications for the position of sub-inspector. For this it appeared that seven were from local men and the others from a distance.

He also read the testimonials of Mr. Lowe, who had been engaged on the Madras Harbour Works and elsewhere.

The Chairman stated that Mr. Jillings had sent no testimonials. Whoever was appointed would be engaged as a weekly servant. Mr. J. Riches, jun., asked Mr. Jarvis if he did not believe in employing local men. The Chairman said he did not believe in favouring one local man as against other local men. If they considered the man who was the best suited the majority of the ratepayers would have nothing to grumble at. In selecting the best man to carry out the work he did not think they would be doing wrong. Their duty was to consider the best interests of the ratepayers.

Mr. G. Riches, jun., proposed the adoption of the committee's report. Mr. J. Bower seconded. Mr. J. Riches, jun., moved an amendment, that Mr. J. Jillings be appointed sub-inspector of the works. On a division there was a tie, seven voting for and seven against the amendment, and the committee's recommendation appointing Mr. Lowe was carried by the casting vote of the Chairman.

A letter was received from Mr. W. Kemp, Cambridge House, with regard to a scheme for supplying music during next season. Mr. J. Riches, jun., proposed that the letter be laid on the table.

Mr. G. Riches, jun. – Won't you help local talent? On the suggestion of the Chairman, it was decided to inform Mr. Kemp that at present the Board were making no arrangements with regard to next season.

The Clerk read a communication from the Board of Trade in which the Department assented to the conveyance to the Commissioners for the sum of £5 and payment of the necessary legal expenses that portion of the foreshore below low water which will be taken by the pier, on the payment of a rental to the Crown of one shilling a year.

The Urban District Council wrote asking for information as to how far back the Commissioners proposed putting the public footpath on the edge of the Marrams.

It was decided to leave this over until the engineer had prepared plans showing how much of the land they would require. On the motion of Mr. Ambrose Burton, seconded by Mr. G. Riches, jun., it was left with the Works Committee to say when Mr. Lowe, the Sub-Inspector, should commence his duties.

**The Norfolk News (Second Sheet):
Saturday 9th December 1899**

A general meeting was held on Wednesday at the Clerk's Office, Church Street, Cromer. Mr. A. E. Jarvis in the chair. There were present Messrs. J. Curtis, R. A. Clarke, H. Rust, J. Lovelace, F. W. Rogers, G. Riches, jun., J. Bower, G. Kennedy, T. Puxley, J. Riches, jun., L. G. Burton, and G. M. Bultitude.

The Clerk reported a credit balance at the bank of £831 1s. 4d., and that during the month rates to the amount of £337 4s. 2d. had been collected.

The payment by R. Allen of £45 11s. 6d. for wages during the past month was confirmed.

On the motion of Mr. J. Riches, jun., seconded by Mr. R. A. Clarke, the following payments were authorised: – Richard Balls, five weeks' salary at 8s., £2; G. Wilkin, for carting, £4 6s.; and Mr. Turner, pile shoes, £12 4s. 3d.

The Works Committee reported that at their meeting held that day the Superintendent of the Works, Mr. Woodford Pilkington, attended, and was instructed to see that the greatest care was taken as to the proportion of sand and shingle taken from the Beach for the new works. The committee recommended that the application of Mr. Thorne, the contractor for the pier, for permission to place his private office on the band stand should be granted. Messrs. Douglass & Arnott, the engineers, under date December 6th, sent in the following report: -

Eastern Section – Messrs. A. Fasey & Son. – The contractors are making fair progress. A second consignment of 60 tons of cement has been delivered, a steam crane set up, temporary tram road, and other plant deposited on the site.

The cement, stone, and superintendent's office are complete, 203 ft. in length of trench has been timbered and excavated, and partly filled in with concrete. A second trench 28 ft. in length has been got out, and partly concreted for pier abutment. Eighty-five workmen are now employed in this section.

Western Section – Messrs. B. Cooke & Co. – Plant is now being delivered on to site.

A cement store has been erected at the Beach Station, and 80 tons of cement placed in store. Messrs. B. Cooke & Co. inform us that they will start operations to-morrow. The work has been set out along the line of walls and bastions.

Promenade Pier – Mr. Thorne. – The wrought iron piles are ready for delivery from Messrs. Head, Wrightson & Co. Eight cast-iron columns are cast, a number of 65-lb. rails delivered, and other materials rolled at the mills. Mr. Thorne is now at Cromer arranging for the erection of shops and offices prior to sending down the work. He anticipates making an early start to drive the iron piles, for which work a new pile-driver is being made. Mr. Lowe, foreman, entered on his duties on Monday, the 27th ult.

On the motion of Mr. Bultitude, seconded by Mr. Rogers, the foregoing reports were adopted, with the addition that Mr. Thorne give up the possession of the bandstand when required by the Commissioners.

The Chairman read another letter from Mr. William Kemp, Cambridge House, re. musical arrangements for next season. He said he had also received other letters on the same subject. He felt that the sooner they made the necessary arrangements for next season the better.

He thought the wisest course would be to leave the whole thing in the hands of the Works Committee to consider and report. On the motion of Mr. T. Puxley, seconded by Mr. G. Kennedy, this was agreed to.

Chapter Four – 1900

The Norwich Mercury: Saturday 6th January 1900

Mr. G. Riches, jun., presided over a meeting of the Protection Commissioners on Wednesday.

The Clerk reported that during the month rates to the amount of £178 11s. had been collected.

R. Allen's report on work on the groyne was received and adopted, and on the motion of Mr. Curtis, seconded by Mr. J. Riches, jun., his wage payments, £35 17s. 8d., for the month were confirmed under date December 30th, 1899.

Messrs. Douglass and Arnott, the engineers for the protection works, reported as follows: -

Eastern Section: Messrs. A. Fasey and Son. – This section is being proceeded with in a satisfactory manner whenever the tides and weather admit of work at the several sections.

The Pier bastion foundations are taken out for a length of over 40 ft. and concreted.

The section of wall adjoining the Hotel de Paris steps, started this month, has the foundation laid for a length of 65 ft. in concrete.

The third section towards the eastern gangway, of which 203 ft. was trenched last month and partly concreted, has been extended to 253 ft. The number of workmen employed during the month has averaged 85. The cement continues to give very satisfactory results under tests.

Western section: Messrs. B. Cooke and Co. – This section was started by the contractors on the 3rd inst., at the Grand Hotel groyne, when the section of trenching showed a good clay bottom. The sea wall foundation trench has been carried to the eastward 315 feet, and concreted. This is still in clay. The cement continues to give satisfactory results. Thirty workmen are employed on this section.

Pier Section: Mr. Alfred Thorne. – The contractor has started operations during the month. A pile driver has been made, and an iron driving stage erected, from which the piles are to be driven. Eight wrought iron built piles have been delivered, and further piles are ready for delivery. A blacksmith's shop has been built on the parade. We have visited the Consett and Wissen iron works, to inspect and test the steel and cast iron before delivery by manufacturers.

At Cromer we find that the steel and cast-iron piles under supply are in all respects equal to the requirements of the specification. We also inspected at Darlington thirty-one cast-iron columns which have been cast and the flanges machined. The work throughout is very satisfactory, both as regards material and workmanship.

The report was adopted.

As recommended by the Works Committee, it was decided to pay travelling expenses to Cromer of Mr. W. Pilkington, superintendent, and Mr. J. H. Lowe.

This was only carried by a majority of one.

On the recommendation of the same committee, it was resolved, that in consideration of the Bond-Cabbell trustees giving immediate possession of the cliff property, included in the notices to treat, to deposit the sum of £500 in the hands of Mr. P. E. Hansell and Mr. E. R. Greenwall, at Messrs. Barclay's Bank, undertake to pay interest at 5 per cent. per annum from the date of possession being given, on the sum eventually awarded as compensation for the property included in the said notices, the compensation to be ascertained in the ordinary course, it being mutually understood that such deposit shall be treated as a security to the trustees on their giving possession, and not as evidence of the value of the property, and shall not be referred to in any proceedings with respect to compensation.

In the course of the discussion Mr. Puxley inquired the idea of such a big sum being asked for as a deposit.

Mr. Rust said originally it was double that, £1,000.

Mr. J. Curtis said they were about to protect property, thereby making it three times more valuable, and yet had to pay for doing so. He did not think it right, and instanced the increased value given to property near the watch house by work done there.

As recommended by the Works Committee, the following payments were authorised: – General bills, £198 5s. 4½d.; Messrs. A. Fasey and Son, on account of contract, as certified by engineers, £1,465 8s. 10d.; Messrs. Douglass and Arnott, engineers (1) commission on above certificate £73 5s. 3d., and (2) commission on reconstruction of jetty groyne £15 16s.

Eastern Daily Press: Thursday 25th January 1900

A special meeting was held yesterday at the Clerk's Office, Church Street, Cromer, Mr. A. E. Jarvis in the chair. There were present Messrs. G. Riches, jun., R. A. Clarke, G. Kennedy, Ambrose Burton, T. Puxley, J. Lovelace, and L. G. Burton.

The Works Committee recommended that the kiosks at the entrance of the pier should be 6 ft., instead of 9 ft. across, and be roofed with zinc tiles.

That the Urban District Council have their attention drawn to the delay in the commencement of the septic tank works. The committee also reported with regard to a band for the season. Mr. W. Kemp of Cromer had handed in certain particulars, and the committee had also been in correspondence with Messrs. Keith, Prowse, & Co., of London. They recommended that arrangements be made with Messrs. Keith, Prowse, & Co. for a concert by the Blue Hungarian Band at an early date, the proceeds, after payment of expenses, to be given to the War Fund.

The Clerk read the following letter received from Messrs. Douglass & Arnott, the engineers: -

15, Victoria Street, Westminster, 23rd January, 1900.

SIR – With reference to the instructions of the Works Committee we have seen Mr. Thorne in the matter of making greater progress with his contract for the construction of the promenade pier, and in particular on the point of delay in driving the piles for want of a suitable dolly.

In former works where the beach was apparently of a similar nature, elm had sufficed for this purpose. We advised Mr. Thorne to use karri wood. The use of this has been the means of getting the two first piles down to their proper level.

A heavy cast-iron driving length is about to go forward to Cromer, so that in case of the failure of the karri wood there will be a suitable dolly on hand.

Mr. Thorne anticipates having the piles in clusters (1) and (2) ready by the time the girders are built. The whole of the steel has been rolled for these girders and the work is proceeding satisfactorily at Messrs. Westwood & Co's. works at Bow.

We are of opinion that more rapid progress will now be made with pile-driving, which is to be proceeded with by hand, unless further difficulty should arise, until the first girders are placed on the columns.

The columns have been cast and machined, but the tie rods are not rolled in consequence of stoppage of the rolls at Smethwick Works, due to scarcity of fuel. The works report under date of yesterday that they will use every endeavour to give delivery of these bars at an early date.

The engineers also sent a copy of a letter written to Messrs. Fasey & Son, the contractors for the eastern section of the protection work: -

Cromer, 23rd January, 1900.

Gentlemen – The Cromer Protection Commissioners instruct us to inform you that the construction of the pier abutment is not being proceeded with as rapidly as is desirable. As you will be aware the pier girders, which are now in course of being made, rest on this abutment, and Mr. Thorne, the contractor for the pier, is anxious to place the first girders in position, as soon as the first bay of piles is driven. Should he not be able in consequence of the abutment not being built, to place his girders, the delay thus caused will be a matter of serious inconvenience, not only to Mr. Thorne, but also to the Commissioners.

We are of opinion that with the exercise of a little more diligence and protection from the wash of the sea, this section of the work should make greater progress.

We must ask you to devote special attention to this point and write us as to what method you will adopt to ensure greater progress being made. – Yours truly, Douglass & Arnott.

On the motion of Mr. G. Riches, jun., seconded by Mr. T. Puxley, all the recommendations of the committee were adopted without discussion.

THE CONSTRUCTION OF CROMER PIER

Eastern Daily Press: Thursday 1st February 1900

> TWO HUNDRED LABOURERS Wanted at Cromer for Seawall and Sewerage Works.— Apply to Cooke, Contractors, Cromer.

Eastern Evening News: Thursday 8th February 1900

A general meeting was held yesterday at the Clerk's Office, Church Street, Cromer. There were present Mr. A. E. Jarvis (Chairman), and Messrs. George Riches, R. A. Clarke, J. Lovelace, F. W. Rogers, and H. Rust.

The Clerk reported a credit balance at the bank of £401 8s. 2d., and that since the last statement was presented rates to the amount of £47 8s. 10d. had been collected. R. Allen's report on the progress of the pile driving on the two groynes east of the town was received and adopted. Wage payments by him to the amount of £45 2s. 6d. for the past five weeks were confirmed.

The Clerk read the following report from Messrs. Douglass & Arnott, the engineers, on the state of the work up to the end of January: -

Eastern Section – Messrs. A. Fasey & Son, the contractors, have under somewhat trying circumstances as to weather and high tides, taken advantage of every opportunity to push forward the trenching and construction of the sea walls and pier abutment. We have advised the firm to make use of clay dams to protect the excavated trenches and foundation walls whilst these are in hand from the sea, and we understand that our advice is being taken in this matter.

The Pier bastion foundations are now deposited in concrete for a length of 155 ft., thus leaving a length of 76 ft. to connect with the old work. The trenching and foundation of walls between Hotel de Paris groyne and eastern gangway have been got out and concreted for a further length of 202 ft. The length of wall remaining to be founded is 110 ft. The amount of work done under this section during the month is £797 1s. 8d., 10 per cent. being deducted for retention.

THE CONSTRUCTION OF CROMER PIER

Western Section – Messrs. B. Cooke & Co., the contractors, are making good progress with the sea walls, this section of the work not being washed by the tides to the same extent as the eastern section.

The wall foundations have been extended to the eastward and westward a further length of 258 ft. 470 ft. run of wall is completed to coping level. The foundations for the stones are being taken out. The first certificate for this section in the sum of £1,464 5s. 3d. is now due to the contractors.

Pier section – Mr. Alfred Thorne. During the month four wrought iron-built piles have been driven into the beach to their full extent, and left ready for the cast iron columns. We have inspected and tested further material before delivery, and find same to be in accordance with the specification.

The cast iron columns, and piers No. 2 and 3 are in course of delivery to Cromer.

The steel for the main girders is now being prepared for riveting up by Messrs. Westwood. The difficulty which was at first met with in driving the iron piles has been overcome by the use of karri wood and cast iron dolleys. The piles are now driven at an average rate of one in two days.

The value of work delivered and erected on this section amounts to £951 4s. 9d., after making the usual deductions.

The Works Committee reported that under date of February 2nd Mr. A. Thorne, the contractor for the pier, wrote attributing delay to the closing of the gangway and the progress made in connection with the pier abutment.

The engineers had been instructed to reply that the Board did not admit that there had been any delay caused to him by the work on the gangway, or the condition of the work on the abutment, or that the Commissioners had any liability.

The committee recommended that as certified by the engineers, payments be made as follows: – Messrs. Cooke & Co., western section, £1,464 5s. 3d.; Mr. A. Thorne, Pier section, £951 4s. 9d. Mr. F. W. Rogers proposed, and Mr. Lovelace seconded the adoption of the report, exclusive of the payment to Mr. Thorne.

The Chairman said the engineers' certificate was for work done and materials delivered. Mr. Rogers said the committee were not satisfied with the way the pier contract work was being done. It was a question whether payment or withholding it would expedite matters.

Mr. Rust said the engineers' advice was to pay down at once. The Chairman said they did not want the contractor to think that by paying him they were satisfied with the progress made.

The motion was then agreed to. Mr. George Riches next moved, and Mr. Lovelace seconded, that the question of Mr. Thorne's payment be adjourned for a week to allow of a detailed statement being presented. This was adopted. The meeting was then adjourned to Wednesday next at 2.30 p.m.

Eastern Evening News: Thursday 15th February 1900 (article 1)

During the storm on Tuesday night the heavy seas played havoc with the timber on the eastern section of the protection work now in progress at Cromer. The pier pile driving apparatus also had its position shifted by the force of the waves.

Eastern Evening News: Thursday 15th February 1900 (article 2)

An adjourned meeting was held yesterday at the Clerk's Office, Church Street, Cromer, Mr. A. E. Jarvis in the chair. There were present Messrs. R. A. Clarke, G. Kennedy, J. Lovelace, Ambrose Burton, J. Bower, H. Rust, F. W. Rogers, T. Puxley, G. M. Bultitude, L. G. Burton, and J. Riches, jun.

On the motion of the Chairman, seconded by Mr. Clarke, the Board placed on record their deep regret at the loss sustained by the town of Cromer in the death of Mr. Geo. Riches, sen., who was for many years a Commissioner, and expressed to Mrs. Riches and family their sincere sympathy in their great bereavement.

On the recommendation of the Works Committee, the following payments on account of contracts, as certified by the engineer, were authorised: – Mr. A. Thorne (Pier section) £951 4s. 9d., and Messrs. Fasey & Son (eastern section) £1,000. This, said the Chairman, made a total to Messrs. Fasey & Son up to date of £2,465 8s. 10d. The contractor had done £1,000 worth of work since the last payment was made.

The Chairman said Mr. Douglass, the engineer, had prepared a scheme for lighting the entire promenade, and also the Pier, with gas. It was proposed to use Loftus lamps.

The original idea was to have the lamps on the rails at the side of the Pier. There part of the light would be on the sea.

It was now suggested that, with the exception of the narrow portion of the Pier, they should be in the centre.

Mr. Douglass will attend the next meeting with regard to the scheme.

The Works Committee recommended that the Clerk should interview Messrs. Keith, Prowse, & Co. of London as to whether they would make the Commissioners an offer for a ten weeks' engagement of the Blue Viennese Band, that performed in Cromer Town Hall last week, to commence about July 8th.

The Chairman said he thought it would be well to hear the report of an expert, who was present at the recent concert. Under date February 10th, Mr. Frank W. B. Noverre, leader and secretary of the Norwich Philharmonic Society wrote: "I attended the concert given by the Blue Viennese Band on Friday night, and was much delighted with the performance. They were one and all accomplished musicians, and their unanimity was perfect, and their style excellent.

I don't hesitate to say that should the Cromer Protection Commissioners see their way to engaging them to play at Cromer for the coming season they will be providing a highly attractive and intellectual entertainment for the visitors to your most charming seaside resort.

Speaking as one who has been mixed up with music all his life and had much experience in instrumental music, I should want no better entertainment than spending a few hours at Cromer and listening to the music of so charming a band, I would suggest that for open air performances they should select louder pieces, and that they should be protected with a screen, and something overhead; also that they should give some concerts twice a week or oftener in your Town Hall, when solos might be performed such as is heard from the bandmaster, Herr Moritz Wurm, who is a violinist of the highest order."

Mr. J. Riches, jun., thought they should consider whether it was a string or brass band that was required.

Mr. G. Kennedy said they did not want a band they could hear all over the town. Mr. J. Riches, jun., thought they should have a military band from Norwich.

The Chairman said had Mr. Riches been on a band committee he would have known more about the subject. He did not consider the bands from Norwich had given satisfaction.

Mr. A. Burton moved the adoption of the committee's recommendation. Mr. Bultitude seconded and the committee's recommendation was adopted.

Eastern Daily Press: Tuesday 20th February 1900

An adjourned meeting was held yesterday at the Clerk's Office, Church Street, Cromer, Mr. A. E. Jarvis in the chair. There were present Messrs. R. A. Clarke, G. Kennedy, J. Lovelace, F. W. Rogers, Ambrose Burton, J. Riches, jun., T. Puxley. Mr. Douglass, the engineer, also attended the meeting.

The Clerk read correspondence that had passed between the Board and Messrs. Keith, Prowse, & Co., of London, with reference to the Blue Viennese Band. The company wrote that they could not provide the band that performed at the war concert, but were willing to supply one, to be conducted by Herr Eder, that was equal to it in every respect.

The band would play twice daily, Sunday excepted, and the price for the ten weeks stated was £56 a week.

The Works Committee recommended that an offer be made for a nine weeks' engagement at the price named, the band to be as above stated, with the possibility of a further two weeks' engagement if the Board desired it.

Mr. F. W. Rogers proposed the adoption of the report. Mr. A. Burton seconded.

Mr. T. Puxley thought that before it was decided to engage a band they should know if the Pier would be ready. He considered a string band of the description they had heard, was an excellent one. But he did not think it was able to perform outside except under cover. Therefore, if it could not play on the Pier under cover it was absolutely useless to them. He wished to know what the engineer had to say as to the progress of the works.

Mr. Douglass said so far as he could see there was no question whatever but that the Pier practically to the head would be finished long before the band came down.

Mr. R. Clarke asked what length of pier would then be completed. Mr. Douglass – About 360 ft. Mr. Puxley, in supporting the committee's recommendation, suggested that a clause should be added that Messrs. Keith, Prowse, & Co. should undertake to change the band if so required by the Commissioners during the specified period. Mr. J. Riches, jun., was of the same opinion, and the committee's report, with this additional clause, was then adopted.

The Works Committee reported that, as asked by them, Mr. A. Thorne had sent in a revised tender for the whole superstructure of the Pier, exclusive of the shelters and seats at the head. This tender, the acceptance of which they recommended, was £2,526.

The Chairman said Mr. Thorne's original tender was £3,741. By leaving over to another year the erection of the now excluded work at the head of the Pier, the tender had been reduced by £1,215. Mr. J. Riches asked why that was done. The Chairman – Simply because they could not exceed the powers they had. On the motion of Mr. Lovelace, seconded by Mr. Rogers, the recommendation was adopted.

Eastern Daily Press: Monday 26th February 1900

Cromer Notes

A landslip of the cliffs at the west end of the Marrams occurred on Friday evening.

The actual spot is near the narrow neck of cliff connecting the Marrams with the Runton cliffs.

Here for a distance of about forty yards, and at varying widths, the cliff has fallen away.

This is the largest fall of cliff to the west of the town that has taken place for some years. In extent it is nothing like so large as the recent landslips on the Lighthouse Hills.

But within no great distance from this last fall, men are at work on the beach with the western section of the sea wall extension. At the time of the fall the work of the day was over.

Eastern Daily Press: Tuesday 27th February 1900

A special meeting of the Protection Commissioners was held yesterday at the Clerk's Office, Church Street, to decide as to the band for the coming season. Mr. A. E. Jarvis presided, and there were present Messrs. J. Lovelace, R. A. Clarke, A. Burton, H. Rust, G. M. Bultitude, J. Riches, jun., F. W. Rogers, J. Bower, and T. Puxley.

The Clerk read a letter from Messrs. Keith, Prowse, & Co., of London, in which they intimated inability to accept the clause with regard to the band as contained in the Board's last letter on the subject.

The Works Committee recommended the engagement of the band, with the clause deleted. Mr. Rogers moved the adoption, and Mr. Bultitude seconded. Mr. T. Puxley proposed, and Mr. J. Riches, jun., seconded, that the band be not engaged. Mr. Puxley held that in view of the objection raised to the clause they had no other course than not to engage the band.

Apart from that, he doubted if the Pier would be ready for use in time. If not where were they to recoup some of their outlay?

The Chairman said assuming for the sake of argument that the Pier was not finished, the Board had power under their new Act to rail off any portion of the Promenade and make a charge if they so desired. As for the band, Messrs. Keith, Prowse, & Co. had promised in their letter, read at the last meeting, to provide one "equal in every respect" to that which performed at the Town Hall.

Mr. Rogers said the Board had done their best to get a good band, and now it was not wanted. Perhaps they had better go on as they had done in past years. Mr. J. Riches, jun., asked if the expert's opinion of the band that came down was voluntary or not. The Clerk said he was paid two guineas. Mr. J. Riches, jun., thought the Chairman said it was voluntary.

The Chairman remarked he stated nothing of the kind. What he said was that a gentleman had written a letter which he then asked the Clerk to read. He said nothing as to whether it was, or was not authorised.

On a vote only two were for the amendment, and the committee's recommendation to engage the band was adopted. A cheque was authorised to be drawn for the payment to Mr. George Middleton of £9 18s. for printing.

A communication from the Urban District Council with regard to the obstructions on the Promenade and top of West Gangway delaying the commencement of the septic tank works, was referred to the Works Committee.

The Norfolk News (First Sheet): Saturday 10th March 1900

A general meeting was held on Wednesday at the Clerk's Office, Church Street, Cromer, Mr. A. E. Jarvis in the chair. There were present Messrs. J. Lovelace, R. A. Clarke, J. Riches, sen., H. Rust, G. Riches, J. Bower, J. Riches, jun., F. W. Rogers, and T. Puxley. Mr. Arnott (Messrs. Douglass & Arnott) also attended the meeting.

The Clerk reported a credit balance at the bank of £370 18s., and that during the month rates to the amount of £41 19s. 11d. had been collected. R. Allen's report on work on the groynes was received and adopted, and wage payments by him to the sum of £37 9s. were confirmed.

Cheques were authorised as follows: – R. Balls, Esplanade Keeper, salary, 32s.; and G. W. Bishop, timber supplied, £25 8s. 7d. The monthly report of the engineers, dated 28th February, was presented by Mr. Arnott.

It ran –

Eastern Section. – Messrs. A. Fasey & Son. The rough weather which prevailed during the early part of the month caused a considerable amount of damage to the contractors' plant, &c., the sea destroying a quantity of shutters and profiles placed against the concrete walls. At the same period portions of the concrete already deposited were washed out. The foundations of the pier abutment have been completed, and the walls carried to an average of 12 ft. above O.D.

The foundations for the Bath Hotel bastion are brought up in concrete to 10 ft. ordnance stratum for 75 ft. and 27 ft. to footing level, leaving 50 ft. of wall not yet executed. The sea wall has been extended to its termination at the western gangway, consequently the entire length of walls under this contract, with the exception of 50 ft. to Bath Hotel bastion, the Paris Hotel incline, and gangway walls, have been founded and carried up to varying heights from 18 to 20 ft. ordnance stratum.

The cast concrete, coping, string courses, mouldings, and pillars are being moulded. The average number of workmen employed is 102.

Western Section. – Messrs. B. Cooke & Co. The work under this section continues to advance satisfactorily. The foundations for the sea wall have been extended in a westerly direction 800 feet during the month, including the formation of two bastions. A length of sea wall of 670 feet is brought up to coping level. A quantity of filling for the cliff has been deposited behind the sea wall, and the wall thus efficiently protected.

A slip of cliff estimated at 400 cubic yards occurred on the 23rd February. The excavations for the sea wall will require to be made through this deposit, the excavated material being partially wheeled back in the form of filling.

The Surveyor has given instructions during the month as to the position of the septic tank walls. Messrs. Cooke consequently re-started operations at the eastern end last week.

By reason of the work being damaged by sea this section was again abandoned, but is now being actively proceeded with. The tunnel in connection with the stores is proceeding satisfactorily.

A quantity of bricks, concrete, steps dressings, &c., is delivered. The workmen employed have averaged 103. At present the number is 107.

Pier Section. – Mr. Alfred Thorne, the contractor, has completed driving the eight piles in the first bay, and removed the piling stage to the second bay.

The number of piles driven this month, amounting to 7, has been small, owing to inclement weather. As soon as the girders and crane are erected the contractor anticipates employing steam. The crane has arrived at the Beach Station. The first bay of cast iron columns has been erected and braced.

We have inspected five of the main girders for the first bay at the works of Messrs. Westwood & Co. of Bow, and passed same. They are in course of delivery. Two more large and a number of small girders are in a forward state. Sixteen tons of steel joists, the whole of the pile shoes, eight wrought iron piles, 28 lengths of cast iron columns, and 1½ tons of tie rods have been delivered. The workmen employed number 17.

The report was adopted, and on the recommendation of the Works Committee the following payments were authorised: – Messrs. Fasey & Son (eastern section), £730 11s. 2d.; Mr. A. Thorne (pier section), £766 3s.; and Messrs. Cooke & Co. (western section), £1,492 19s. 3d.; and Messrs. Douglass & Arnott (commission), £170 15s. 6d.

Inclusive of the above instalments, the total payments made to the contractors up to date is: Eastern section, £3,196; pier section, £1,717 7s. 9d. and western section, £2,957 4s. 3d.

The Clerk reported that the next election of Commissioners would take place on 2nd May.

This was a month later than under the old system, and for the first time the voting would be by ballot. The five seats to be filled up were those of Messrs. J. Jillings, J. Bower, G. Kennedy, T. Fowell Buxton, and J. Riches, sen.

On the motion of Mr. Rogers, seconded by Mr. Rust, a cheque for £300 was ordered to be drawn towards the cost of the Protection Act. The Clerk, in reply to Mr. J. Riches, jun., said £250 had already been paid, making £550 in all. He hoped at an early date to present a full statement of the expenses incurred.

The Norfolk News: Saturday 7th April 1900

A general meeting was held on Wednesday at the Clerk's Office, Church Street, Cromer, Mr. A. E. Jarvis in the chair. There were present Messrs. R. A. Clarke, J. Riches, sen., H. Rust, G. Kennedy, J. Bower, G. M. Bultitude, F. W. Rogers, T. Puxley, and J. Riches, jun. Mr. Arnott (Messrs. Douglass & Arnott) also attended.

The Clerk reported a credit balance at the bank of £547 16s. R. Allen's wage payments, to the amount of £41 9s. 6d., were confirmed. The collectors' statement showed that £26 13s. 2d. had been collected in rates since the last meeting, leaving a sum of £67 7s. 11d. recoverable.

The Clerk, in reply to questions, said it was possible that of the sum returned as recoverable £22 16s. 3d. might be classed as irrecoverable.

Of the reduced sum of £44 11s. 8d., two items, equal to about £14, were still in dispute, leaving a balance of £30 made up of small items.

The report was adopted, and on the motion of Mr. Rogers, seconded by Mr. Bower, it was decided to take legal proceedings against the defaulters.

The Works Committee recommended the acceptance of Messrs. Lewellen's tender, £972 18s., for gas lighting on the front. This was agreed to after a slight criticism from Mr. T. Puxley as to the advisability of expending such a sum on gas lighting when the Urban District Council were proceeding with an electric lighting scheme for the town.

The Chairman said the whole question had been before the Commissioners, who had decided on gas. It was further resolved on the recommendation of the Works Committee to accept Messrs. W. E. Constable & Co's. tender of £1,350 for tar paving the promenades. The engineer's report for the month, read by Mr. Arnott and adopted, was as follows: -

Eastern Section: Messrs. A. Fasey & Son. The contractors, have completed the front wall of the Pier abutment as far as is possible pending the erection of the main girders forming the first bay of the promenade pier. The east wing of the abutment has been carried up to the level of the bull nosing.

On the west wing the walls have been completed, upon the average, to within 3 ft. of the normal parade level.

The east parade wall has been carried up to promenade level for a length of about 1,300 ft., whilst 30 ft. run of this wall still awaits the laying of foundations.

The number of men at present employed upon the section is 111.

The total value of work upon this section, which has been certified for to date amounts to £4,015 16s., being nearly one-half of the contract sum.

Western Section: Messrs. B. Cooke & Co. A length of 1,416 ft. of the parade wall has been completed to coping level, together with 160 ft. of the wall forming the junction with the existing parade; 6,155 cubic yards of filling has been deposited, including a portion from the excavation for the septic tanks. The stores and urinal building is making satisfactory progress, and the tunnel has been driven for a distance of 18 ft.

Work upon the extreme west end of this section has been suspended for the present, in accordance with the instructions of the committee. At the present time 84 men are employed upon the section.

The value of work certified to date is £5,845 19s., nearly half of the contract sum, including the portion of the section to be completed in 1901.

Pier Section: Mr. Alfred Thorne. The second bay of the pier has been fitted with the three main girders, together with the small cross girders and 11 deck joists.

The erection of the crane is in progress, and the piling stage has been removed to the No. 3 pile cluster.

The girders for the first bay have been fitted with sole plates and abutment gussets preparatory to erection in place, and the bracing to the second bay has been completed. Twenty-seven men are at work on this contract.

Work to the value of £3,412 16s. 2d. has been certified for to date, the contractors' sum being in this case £11,275. A large quantity of further material has been delivered in connection with this section during the month.

On the recommendation of the Works Committee, and certified by the engineers, the payment of £2,336 9s. 3d. to Messrs. Cooke & Co. on account of their contract for the western section was authorised. And the payment of £149 to Messrs. Douglass & Arnott, the engineers, as commission on same was also approved. The Works Committee reported efforts they had made to have the work on the eastern and pier sections expedited, and on the motion of Mr. F. W. Rogers, seconded by Mr. T. Puxley it was resolved to postpone until next meeting the payments to the contractors, Messrs. Fasey & Son and Mr. A. Thorne, respectively.

On the recommendation of the Finance Committee Mr. H. P. Gould, of Norwich, was appointed to audit the accounts of the Board for the year 1899, at a sum not exceeding 10 guineas. The following payments were authorised: – Messrs. Bishop, timber, £58 17s. 1d., and spikes, £13 19s.; also R. Balls, four weeks' salary, 32s.

The Clerk read a letter from Major H. A. Barclay regretting that he was unable to attend the meeting of the Board by reason of his military duties.

The Norfolk News (Second Sheet): Saturday 28th April 1900

Norfolk coast fishermen obtained few fish on their lines, and this has been the cause of them having a hard winter. Many of the Cromer fishermen found employment on the new sea wall and pier, but at Sheringham and other places the men were not so fortunate, and had it not been for the heavy catches of lobsters last autumn, they would no doubt have felt the winter even more keenly.

Norfolk Museums Service, Cromer Museum, CRRMU : 1981.80.863
Cromer Pier under construction

THE CONSTRUCTION OF CROMER PIER

The Norfolk News (Second Sheet): Saturday 5th May 1900

A general meeting was held on Wednesday at the Clerk's Office, Church Street, Cromer, Mr. A. E. Jarvis in the chair. There were present Messrs. R. A. Clarke, H. Rust, A. Burton, G. Riches, J. Smith, H. A. Barclay, F. W. Rogers, G. M. Bultitude, J. Bower, J. Riches, jun., L. G. Burton, and J. Lovelace. Mr. Douglass (Messrs. Douglass & Arnott, engineers) also attended.

The Clerk reported a credit balance at the bank of £419 19s. 2d. During the month rates to the amount of £10 5s. 2d. had been received by the collector. R. Allen's report on work done on groynes was adopted. His wages payments, to the total of £42 1s. 6d., were confirmed.

The engineer having called attention to the necessity under the provisions of the Act for a pier-head light, the Clerk was directed to write to the Board of Trade on the subject.

On the recommendation of the Works Committee, Messrs. McDowall, Steven & Co's., (London) tender of £374 for bandstand was accepted. As certified by the engineers, the following payments were authorised: – Messrs. A. Fasey & Son, eastern section, £1,150; Mr. A. Thorne, pier section, £300; Mr. A. Thorne, pier superstructure, £384.

On the recommendation of the Works Committee the payment to the engineers of their commission on work previously certified was also authorised. Bills to the amount of £56 5s. 6d. were ordered to be paid.

The plan submitted by the engineers for sloping the cliff was, on the motion of Mr. Barclay, seconded by Mr. Lovelace, approved.

The men at work under R. Allen on the groyne extension having applied for a fixed wage of 30s. per week, the Board decided to give them a wage of 6d. per hour. On the recommendation of the Finance Committee, it was resolved to give to the Clerk to the Board £40 extra remuneration for his services – for 1899, for the period after the passing of the Act, £10, and for the present year, £30. On the motion of Mr. Barclay, seconded by Mr. Smith, the seal of the Board was ordered to be affixed to the conveyance of the foreshore from the Board of Trade, and the payment to the Department of the sum of £4 4s. was authorised. Mr. Alfred Burton was re-appointed collector of rates on the motion of Mr. Clarke, seconded by Mr. Bower.

THE CONSTRUCTION OF CROMER PIER

Mr. Douglass read the engineer's report of the work on the front. It was as follows:

Eastern Section. – Messrs. A. Fasey & Son. The filling behind the walls has been completed from the Beach House to the Bath Hotel bastion. At the pier abutment some 200 cubic yards of material are still required to be deposited and the surface levelled. 270 feet run of walling below the lifeboat gangway and the pier abutment are ready for the coping and 190 ft. of the channel way completed.

The hand packed filling under the concrete deck has been started. One hundred cubic yards of this has been laid in front of the Tucker's Hotel. The work in connection with the gangway has made steady progress, the new storm overflow being finished to within thirty feet of the junction. The pitching is in progress, and half of the lifeboat slip completed.

The Beach House steps are ready for the brick nosing, and the Bath Hotel bastion has been carried up to 22-69 O.D. The weather during the latter part of the month has been favourable, and a good portion of overtime has been worked.

The number of men employed on this section at the end of the month was ninety, including the contractor's local staff. The total amount of work on this section for which payment has been certified to date is £5,346.

Western Section. – Messrs. B. Cooke & Co. Six hundred and ninety feet run of the parade from the Grand Hotel bastion has the filling placed in position for an average breadth of 15 ft. An area of about 4,000 super yards beyond the approach bastion has the filling levelled up and awaits the hand packed filling and concrete deck. The entire length of this section which has been under construction, together with the slips and the parapet wall of the approach bastion, are ready for coping.

The concrete walls for the slips near the approach bastion are in progress.

At the new central bastion, the walls have been carried up to a height of 7 feet above the footings. The foundations for the store and urinals are in progress. The number of men at present employed upon this section is comparatively small, fifty at the end of the month. This reduction has been made by the contractors pending a decision as to the cliff slopes. The value of work certified to date is £5,293 13s. 6d.

No certificate is being handed in for payment this month.

Pier Section. – Mr. A. Thorne. The first bay of the pier has been laid with deck joists and the wind screens under seats fixed. The pile driving at cluster No. 3 has been finished and the engine removed to No. 4 cluster, the driving of which is in progress.

Four columns and two girders are in place at cluster No. 3. A sufficient quantity of steel and iron work has been delivered to date, and a supply of timber for decking, &c., has arrived. More satisfactory progress has been made with this section during the past month than previously.

The number of men employed has been largely increased, at the end of the month the men being 43.

The steam gear for the piling engine has enabled more rapid progress to be made with the driving latterly. The value of work certified to date is £3,393 12s. 5d.

We have inspected further sections of the work at the several manufactories where the same is under manufacture, and find the supply of material to be in a forward state.

Pier superstructure. – Mr. Alfred Thorne. The kiosks and shelters are well in hand and are expected to be delivered on the work during the latter part of May.

The gates, stanchions, lamp-posts, &c., are in hand, and a number of the seat frame castings have been deposited. The contractor expects to have a further supply of these and other castings sent off immediately.

Gas Mains and Parade Lighting. – Messrs. Lewellen & Co. The work has been set out and the position of the lamp-posts determined on the eastern section as far as the Beach House. The mains have been laid and covered in at the eastern end as far as the crossing of the east gangway.

The whole of the cast iron main has been delivered and placed in position alongside the work. It is expected that the mains will be laid as far as Tucker's Hotel by 5th inst. The lamp-posts, &c., are in hand, and will be delivered this month. Eight men have been employed on this work.

The annual meeting of the Council for the election of Chairman and Vice-Chairman takes place on Wednesday, May 16th.

*Norfolk Museums Service, Cromer Museum, CRRMU : 1981.78.8
Cromer's eastern promenade*

Eastern Daily Press: Saturday 2nd June 1900

THE CROMER PIER
To the Editor

SIR – Having lately arrived as a resident in Cromer, and being much interested in the work now in progress in connection with the new Pier, I would like, through the medium of your columns, to draw attention to a little matter which I have often noticed, and which strikes me as capable of some improvement.

I allude to the masonry abutment of the pier, which has been constructed with a flat face.

The effect of this is that at high tide waves rolling in fall against this flat face, rebound straight back off it, and meet succeeding in-flowing waves roughly about 30 to 50 feet from the abutment, and that when these two waves, rolling and breaking in opposite and parallel directions, meet, a mass of water is shot straight up into the air to a considerable height and with no inconsiderable force against the superstructure and flooring of the Pier.

This may, at first blush, appear a matter of but small moment, but just as dropping water will wear away a stone, so I cannot help thinking that, as time goes on, this continual upward beating of the water will gradually but surely tend not only to strain and weaken the superstructure, but also, perhaps, to loosen the foundations of the iron pile-driven piers themselves; and it is therefore, in my humble opinion, a material factor and worthy of some consideration in calculating upon the stability and length of life of the new Pier.

The danger could be minimised, if not obviated entirely, by the addition of a little concrete to the face of the abutment to break it into a salient instead of leaving it straight. The rebound would then be to either side, and clear of the superstructure, instead of directly under it, as at present, and a few extra pounds expended in this direction now may mean the saving of a good many in repairs later on.

I have not yet had an opportunity of witnessing the effect of an exceptional high tide accompanied with a northerly gale, but the usual normal conditions are quite bad enough.

My opinion is, of course, only that of a layman, but it is quite possible that there may be something in it for all that. – I remain, yours faithfully,

F. A. C., Lieut. – Colonel. The Norfolk Army College, May 31st 1900.

Eastern Daily Press: Friday 8th June 1900

Notice to Mariners

ENGLAND—EAST COAST.

TEMPORARY LIGHT AT THE END OF CROMER PIER WORKS.

THE CROMER PROTECTION COMMISSIONERS Hereby give Notice that on the 30th day of June, 1900, a FIXED RED LIGHT will be Exhibited from Sunset to Sunrise at the Sea End of the Cromer Pier Construction Works.

By Order, P. E. HANSELL,

Clerk to the Cromer Protection Commissioners.

Cromer, 7th June, 1900.

The Norfolk News (First Sheet): Saturday 9th June 1900

CROMER PROTECTION
COMMISSIONERS

PROGRESS OF THE NEW WORKS

A meeting of this Board was held on Wednesday at the Clerk's Office, Church Street, Cromer, Mr. A. E. Jarvis in the chair. There were present Messrs. H. Rust, G. M. Bultitude, J. Lovelace, R. A. Clarke, J. W. Jefferson, A. C. Savin, J. Bower, F. W. Rogers, A. Burton, G. Riches, J. Riches, jun., and Mr. W. Churchyard.

The Clerk reported a credit balance at the bank of £286 17s. 8d. R. Allen's report of work done on groynes, &c., was received, and wage payments by him to the amount of £55 16s. for the month were confirmed. The report, dated June 1st, of Messrs. Douglass & Arnott, the engineers, as to the work on the sea front was as follows: -

Eastern Section, Messrs. Fasey & Son. – The gangway, toe pitching, and lifeboat gangway concreting are complete. The promenade between the gangway and the Bath Hotel, including railings, steps, parapet, and preparation for tar-paving is practically complete.

The promenade wall between the Bath Hotel and Pier abutment wing wall has been brought forward to coping level and the filling behind made up to about surface level. The promenade slip extension wall has been formed and built for a length of 60 feet.

The Pier abutment has been filled to within a foot of finished level, bull-nosed coping, parapet wall, entrance pillars, steps and retaining walls brought forward for completion. An average of 80 workmen has been employed. Good progress has been made on this section during the month. Beyond a general clearing and preparation for tar-paving little work remains to complete the contract.

Western Section, Messrs. B. Cooke & Co. – Considerable delay has been occasioned on this section, in consequence of the septic tanks underlying a section of the promenade not having been completed. The arches were out of hand last week, thus enabling the filling over same to be proceeded with. About 550 lineal feet of path scarping cutting has been carried out to the cliffs.

One hundred lineal feet of wall coping is, and 400 lineal feet cast in readiness for setting. The new bastion on the old promenade has been constructed to promenade level. This has been flint faced to correspond with the adjacent wall.

The two slips leading to beach have been filled with sand to coping level. The stores and lavatory have been brought forward to receive girders. The average number of workmen employed has been 55.

Last week the number employed was 75. A considerable amount of work still remains to be done before the promenades can be tar paved. The opening out of a section of the promenade between the septic tanks and the pier abutment will further delay completion. Arrangements have been made to remove the contractor's sheds as occasion may arrive.

Pier: Section 1. – Mr. A. Thorne. The piles in cluster No. 4 have been driven, and the pile driver removed to start cluster 5. Bays Nos. 3 and 4, girders, columns, struts, and tie rods have been erected, and the floor joists placed thereon. Material continues to arrive from manufacturers in sufficient consignments.

The pier has been decked over for the first two bays – 100 ft., and seat chairs, rail stanchions, rails, wind screen erected.

Section 2. – The material for completing the first section of the superstructure is in a forward condition when not delivered.

The contractor has been delayed for some days by inclement weather and high seas, which latter prevented the pile-driving being pushed on. Forty workmen have been continuously employed.

Gas Mains and Parade Lighting – Messrs. Lewellen & Co. The mains have been laid between the lifeboat gangway and septic tanks, and a further length to the westward of these tanks.

The lamps and connections have all been completed to Eastern Parade. A few posts are erected between the gangway and the Bath Hotel. On the Western Parade four lamp-posts are in place and connections in hand to gas main in Runton Road. The contractors are taking every advantage of the work as completed to push forward this section. The contractors have nine men on the work.

The report was adopted. The Works Committee recommended the payment of the following instalments as certified by the engineers: – Eastern section: Messrs. Fasey & Son, £1,312; western section, Messrs. B. Cooke & Co., £1,500; Pier section, Mr. A. Thorne, (a) pile structure, £1,662 10s. 1d., and (b) superstructure, £253 10s. 6d.; gas main section, Messrs. Lewellen & Co., £300; engineers' commission on instalments, exclusive of the above, £130.

The Chairman said Messrs. Fasey & Son had about £800 further work to complete their contract, and that, with the 10 per cent. retention money held by the Board, made about £1,500 still to come to them.

Mr. F. W. Rogers proposed the adoption of the committee's report exclusive of the payment of £130 to the engineers. This, he thought, might stand over for awhile. The Works Committee had tried to expedite matters, and if they could not refuse payment to the contractors their only way was to withhold it from the engineers.

The Chairman – You mean until the next meeting?

Mr. Rogers – Yes.

Mr. J. W. Jefferson seconded the motion, which was carried.

On the recommendation of the Works Committee it was decided, in order to allow of the passage of more beach, to remove two planks from the third to the sixth and one plank from the second to the third stay at the shore end of the western groyne.

The same committee was authorised to do any necessary renovation to seats and rails on the front. On the motion of Mr. A. Burton, seconded by Mr. G. M. Bultitude, the Works Committee was re-elected. An amendment, proposed by Mr. J. Riches, jun., and seconded by Mr. J. Lovelace, that members be elected individually was defeated, only two voting for it. The Finance Committee was then re-appointed, on the motion of Mr. Bultitude, seconded by Mr. Churchyard.

The Chairman drew attention to boats on the west gangway being in the way of Messrs. B. Cooke & Co., the contractors, and to the owners not removing them when requested. On the motion of Mr. Bower, seconded by Mr. Rogers, the Clerk was instructed to take the necessary steps to see to their removal. Bills to the amount of £12 7s. 8d. were ordered to be paid, and the meeting was adjourned to Wednesday, 27th June. On that day the rate for the ensuing year will be made.

The Daily Telegraph: Friday 22nd June 1900

CROMER

At present the sea front promenades are in a state of chaos, but in the course of a few days we are promised a much improved state of affairs. Arrangements have been made for the Blue Viennese Band to commence performances early in July on a portion of the new pier, which is to be finished by June, 1901.

In many ways the town is developing a more go-ahead policy than has heretofore obtained here. Now that bands have not to be provided by voluntary subscriptions the energy of townsfolk might be directed towards providing some form of amusement, for the visitor keenly feels the lack of occupation during the day-time.

During the past few days, the weather has proved showery. The sunsets have been of marvellous beauty, and are watched nightly by large numbers.

The Essex Guardian: Saturday 23rd June 1900

There are great improvements in hand at Cromer. A handsome new pier is already half-built, new promenades are being constructed, and old ones widened, so that in a few months the older residents will hardly know the front.

The pity of it is that whenever there is work to be done at Cromer, it is in progress far into the season, when navvies and bricklayers, carpenters and rivetters, ought, by all rules of common-sense and expediency, to have disappeared.

The Daily Telegraph: Friday 29th June 1900

CROMER

Cold and breezy as was the early part of the week, visitors continued to arrive in large numbers, and there is now promise that the weather has set for fair.

Unfortunately, though the sands are at the visitors' disposal, the promenades facing the town proper are still blocked by workmen, but on

Sunday it appears that the fine, newly-constructed eastern walk will be at their disposal, together with the neatly-designed pier entrance.

A week or so must elapse before the formal sanction of the Board of Trade as to the safety of the structure will be given.

Of the continued fashionable character of the town, notwithstanding the bad state during the month of the sea front, there can be no doubt by the present number of visitors. Golfing naturally claims a great deal of attention, but boating, driving, swimming, &c., claim their fair number of votaries, mixed bathing especially being greatly appreciated.

Trains. – St. Pancras, 10.00 a.m., 1.30 p.m.; return 5.22 p.m., 8.20 p.m.

The Downham Market Gazette: Saturday 30th June 1900

A special meeting was held on Wednesday, Mr. A. E. Jarvis presiding. The estimates for the year were presented by the Finance Committee. They recommended a rate of 1s. 8d. in the £.

Mr. Curtis remarked on the increase in the rate. The Clerk repeated what he said some time ago, that an expenditure of £30,000 would not make any difference to the existing rate. The Commissioners had, however authorised work involving an outlay of £45,000.

The Chairman said all work done had been sanctioned by the full Board. The rise in the price of materials before the time the estimates were got out and contracts signed, and especially the extra piece of work carried out, had increased the expenditure.

The Clerk said if ever there was a year when the estimate must be slightly doubtful it was this year. For one thing, it was impossible to say what the Pier would bring in. The estimate included, among others, a sum of £504 for the band. The report was adopted.

The Works Committee recommended the abandonment on the West Cliff of the proposed east terrace path in consequence of the engineers finding it impossible to retain in some places a 15 ft. path on the top of the cliff. The committee further recommended that the west terrace path should be connected to the Esplanade on the west as well as on the east side. They also reported that the engineer had been instructed to see that the sheds on the Esplanade were removed by next Saturday.

With regard to the Pier they recommended a fixed scale of charges for admission.

For each person 2d. a time, perambulator 4d., and bath chair 6d.; also, that books containing seven tickets for 1s. and 15 for 2s. be supplied, but that no day or season tickets be issued this year. The committee also recommended that Richard Balls be Pier Keeper at 32s. per week for the season, and that ex police-constable Babbage be appointed his successor at 32s. per week to look after the promenades; also, that W. H. Neal be money-taker at the entrance gates at 17s. per week, and all the appointments subject to the approval of the Pier by the Board of Trade.

The Chairman said the Pier Keeper's duties would begin at 6.30 a.m. and finish at 10.15 p.m.

The seal of the Board was ordered to be affixed to the agreement with Messrs. Barclay, Limited, for £30,000 at 3½ per cent.

Mr. G. Riches drew attention to the need for two more steps at the central approach to the Pier. On the motion of Mr. Curtis, seconded by Mr. R. A. Clarke, the Works Committee were authorised to invite an estimate for the work from the contractors, and given power to accept or reject the same.

The Essex Guardian: Saturday 30th June 1900

AN OUT OF DATE ARTICLE

Sir, – I regularly read your paper, and generally feel, after doing so, that I am well-informed of all local events. For a change, last week, however, I bought a copy of your Ilford contemporary, and, under the heading, "Holiday Haunts," are notes on Cromer, which, to say the least, are amusing. It says: "The pier is a poor one, a kind of wooden jetty, and an eyesore to the place."

As a visitor to Cromer two years running, I am able to put right Mr. Frankford by informing him the sea saw fit to remove his eyesore over three years ago, and there is now a beautiful new pier, which is to be extended as far again into the sea at the end of the present season. Then, again, the article proceeds to say, "Mundesley is situated eight miles from Cromer, and can be reached by bus, tourists alighting at North Walsham."

What about the new railway to Mundesley that has been in existence from North Walsham these two years? Ah, Mr. Frankford, when writing about your next "Holiday" take my advice, and get an up-to-date guide before obtaining copy for "Holiday Haunts." Your "last visit," mentioned in the article, must have been about four years ago!

Cromer Crab.
Ilford.
June 23rd, 1900.

P.S. – Since writing above, I have seen a copy of last week's "Guardian," and notice that, by a singular coincidence, Cromer and Mundesley are also dealt with by you.

I am glad to see that the inaccuracies referred to in my letter are not repeated in your article. – C. C.

Norfolk Museums Service, Cromer Museum, CRRMU : 1981.80.866
Cromer Pier from the west promenade

Eastern Daily Press: Friday 6th July 1900

A general meeting was held on Wednesday at the Clerk's Office, Church Street, Cromer, Mr. A. E. Jarvis in the chair. There were present Messrs. J. Curtis, J. Lovelace, H. Rust, J. Riches, jun., T. Puxley, J. W. Jefferson, A. C. Savin, R. A. Clarke, F. W. Rogers and W. Churchyard. Messrs. Douglass and Arnott, the engineers, also attended the meeting.

The Clerk reported a debit balance at the bank of £23 17s. 6d., and that during the month rates to the amount of £31 19s. 4d. had been received by the collector. R. Allen's report as to work on groynes and promenade was presented, and wage payments by him to the total of £42 3s. 3d. were confirmed.

On the motion of Mr. J. Riches, jun., seconded by Mr. Curtis, it was decided to take legal proceedings against the Cromer Water Works for recovery of rates. The engineers' report, under date of 30th June, was read by Mr. Douglass.

Eastern Section. – Messrs. Fasey & Son. The work included in this section has practically been brought to a close, with one exception, viz., the formation of the inclines leading to the beach from the promenade. The coping for the sea wall from the Bath Hotel to the western side of pier abutment has been coped, with the exception of a short length on the abutment, and the old sea wall intervening stuccoed.

The balance of the sand filling has been deposited at two points in front of Tucker's Hotel and pier abutment. The hard filling and concrete and surfacing has been carried forward from the Bath Hotel to the centre of pier approach.

The two inclines leading to the pier gates have been paved in situ with concrete.

The two flights of steps leading from the promenade to the foreshore have been brought forward, and are within measurable distance of completion.

The inclines to the foreshore are under construction. The contractors' cement store and plant are in course of removal. The offices and other items will be cleared off in course of a week. An average of 75 workmen has been employed. In course of ten days the parade between the gangway and pier, with the exception of the inclines previously referred to, will be complete and left in a satisfactory condition.

Western Section. – Messrs. B. Cooke & Co. The filling under parade level has been continued, and is practically completed between the Grand Hotel and approach bastions. The hard filling has been brought forward and completed from the Grand Hotel bastion to the foot of approach, and a section of concrete surfacing laid 20 ft. in width between the above-mentioned bastion and the approach.

The width of hard filling and surfacing will be completed to the shelter in the course of a week. The promenade coping is now set between the Grand Hotel and approach bastion, and the parapet wall practically completed without its coping to its junction with the old sea wall. The approach and centre bastions are in course of completion.

The two slipways are ready for surfacing with the exception of a short length of coping which remains to be set. The stores have made more progress during the month, with one exception, the window and door head arches are turned and the girders placed for the roof concrete. The approach steps are in hand.

The concrete retaining wall, forming the beach approach, and the back retaining wall of the promenade under the cliff are well advanced. No filling has been done to the approach.

The contractor's sheds have been removed to the western end. The septic tank outfall sewer has been laid along the front promenade for the District Council during the month.

A considerable amount of work still remains to be completed under this contract between the pier and the Grand Hotel bastion before this section can be opened to the public. An average of ninety workmen has been employed.

Pier Section. – Mr. A. Thorne. The piles forming cluster five have been driven, and the columns placed thereon. The main and small girders, braces, straps and tie rods have been erected.

During a heavy sea the contractor's stage and pile drivers were unfortunately overturned and the pile engines destroyed. A new pile engine has been made. This should be at work on No. 6 cluster within a week.

The decking of the Pier has been continued from cluster 2 to cluster 4, and sound screen erected.

Section II. – The seats, chairs, battens, and railings have been set up and fixed between clusters 2 and 4.

The two entrance kiosks and two sound screens have been framed and nearly covered in. The entrance gates, turnstiles, and lamp posts are erected. An average of fifteen workmen has been employed on these sections.

Gas Mains and Parade Lighting. – Messrs. Lewellen & Co. The gas mains are completed with the exception of the approach and stores branches. Practically the whole of the lamp posts and lanterns are erected along the promenades, and awaiting the arrival of the burners to complete. The connection and lamps to approach stores, including connections to gas mains, will be undertaken next week.

The report concluded with a reference to the tar paving and the erection of the band stand.

The Works Committee recommended the following payments to contractors as certified by the engineers: – Messrs. Fasey & Son, eastern section £572; Mr. A. Thorne, Pier section 1 £214, Section 2 £884 8s.; Messrs. Lewellen, gas mains, &c., £300; Messrs. Cooke & Co., western section, £1,096. The committee also recommended the payment to the engineers of their commission on the above and previous month's certificates, viz., for June £131 14s., July £251 3s.

On the motion of Mr. Churchyard, seconded by Mr. Clarke, the report was adopted.

The following payments were also authorised: – Mr. Pilkington, superintendent of the protection works, salary, 37 weeks at £4 4s., and Mr. J. H. Lowe, 30 weeks at £2. The latter was also allowed 30s. for overtime.

On the motion of Mr. Curtis, seconded by Mr. J. Riches, jun., payment of £211 8s. 8d. to Messrs. Barclays, Limited, interest on loan for the half-year, was directed. The Chairman said the Board had drawn £23,000 out of the £30,000 the bank had agreed to advance.

The engineers were instructed to press Messrs. Constable & Co. to put on more men for the tar paving.

Subject to its inspection and approval by the Board of Trade, it was decided that the opening of the completed portion of the Pier should take place on Monday week, July 16th, on which day the band performances will also commence.

The Morning Leader (London): Friday 13th July 1900

CROMER

With the second week of this month the life and movement of the season became much more evident. Next week will see the completed portion of the new pier opened to the public. This will make a very attractive promenade. From next Monday the Blue Viennese Band engaged for the season will commence its morning and evening performances.

THE CONSTRUCTION OF CROMER PIER

Opening of Cromer Pier: Monday 16th July 1900

Norfolk Museums Service, Cromer Museum, CRRMU : 2011.31.11

"Opening of new Pier at Cromer, showing gates about to be opened. The group on the pier are the Cromer Protection Commissioners making final examination before declaring pier open".

East Anglian Daily Times: Tuesday 17th July 1900

CROMER'S NEW PIER

During the summer of 1898 the Cromer Protection Commissioners considered the advisability of giving better accommodation, in the form of sea parades, a promenade pier, etc., to the many visitors who made Cromer their headquarters during the summer months. This fact arose owing to the great loss the town felt by the old jetty being swept away by the November gale of 1897.

Plans were prepared embracing the widening of the old promenade between the lifeboat gangway and the approaches leading to the Hotel de Paris, the extension of the existing promenade from the Runton Road toward the west, with bastions, slips, etc. These promenades were given a width of at least 40 feet.

THE CONSTRUCTION OF CROMER PIER

In addition, a promenade pier was to be erected, 500 feet in length, 40 feet in width, with an enlarged head, and fitted with kiosks, ornamental gates, shelters, band stand, seats, etc., with a spacious approach from the promenade.

With this object in view, the Commissioners went to Parliament for an Act empowering them to carry out the work, and the same having been passed, practically unopposed, tenders for the different work were considered in October, 1899; and then followed instructions to the engineers (Messrs. Douglass and Arnott, of Westminster), to proceed with (1), the promenade pier; (2), the promenade between the lifeboat gangway and the pier approach; (3), the promenade between the western end of the old promenade, under the Runton Road approach and the end of the Marrams, a length of 1,760 feet. Simultaneously the Urban Council have been laying down a new system of sewage disposal, and in every respect the town is now up-to-date.

The entrance to the pier has been neatly designed, and the sea front now is one of the most elegant to be found along the coast. As it was practically impossible to complete the whole of the pier, the structure has only been completed to the first head, half-way, and here shelters and a band stand have been erected, and on Monday the celebrated Blue Viennese Band commenced a ten weeks' engagement.

This band has been engaged at a cost of over £500, so that it will be seen no expense is being spared to suit the taste of patrons of this health resort. On Monday the Chairman of the Commissioners formally opened the pier, and in doing so expressed the opinion that the sea front of Cromer was second to none in England.

The portion of the pier opened that day was some thousand feet square larger than the old jetty, but next year at that time the whole of the structure would be completed. He trusted that a larger number of visitors would be attracted by the work done. Amid applause the turnstiles were then unlocked, and visitors perambulated the structure.

The Morning Post: Tuesday 17th July 1900

NEW PIER AT CROMER. – The first half of the new pier at Cromer was opened yesterday. The structure will cost £12,000 when finished. It is part of a comprehensive scheme for beautifying Cromer and protecting it from the encroachment of the sea, the Commissioners being authorised by Parliament to expend £45,000 on the work.

The Norwich Mercury: Wednesday 18th July 1900

A seaside resort that aims at popularity must make the improvement of the sea-front its chief aim. Cromer has realised this. The Urban District Council has done and is doing its best for the improvement of the town generally, while the Cromer Protection Commissioners have improved the sea front almost beyond recognition.

Their work is of public benefit in more ways than one. Its most important aspect, perhaps, is that of protection. For centuries the sea has at intervals swept away huge masses of cliff, and the primary consideration of the Commissioners was to prevent a recurrence of this. How far they have succeeded time alone will prove, for the strength of a raging sea is almost incalculable.

Nevertheless, to all appearances, the sea front of Cromer is now amply protected from further encroachment. The groynes have done much towards raising the level of the beach, and preventing that dreaded scour of the tide which has so greatly tended towards the denudation of the foreshore. Happily, the experiment seems to have been a success. Even now one of the groynes is being extended further seawards.

The protection works and promenade are now about a mile in length. They may conveniently be divided into the eastern and western, and Pier sections. The eastern section, for which Messrs. Anthony Fasey & Son, Leytonstone, were the contractors, is now practically complete. A section of this – from Doctor's Steps to the Beach House – including a pretty and convenient shelter, somewhat like the kiosk in Chapel Field, Norwich, was finished last year, and has been available for visitors while the other works were in progress.

An iron railing extends along the seaward edge of this promenade. The lower portion of the Lifeboat slip has been concreted, and the promenade from the Pier approach to Beach House sloped down so that visitors may cross the Lifeboat slip with comfort.

This promenade has been more than doubled in width, and is approximately 1,900 ft. long and 40 ft. wide. The foundations of the sea wall are about 10 ft. below the beach level and 10 ft. in width. Concrete is utilised everywhere.

The wall is finished off at the top with one foot half-round coping. At intervals along the front there are semi-circular bastions projecting towards the sea. At present these contain seats, but it is possible that at some future date they will be utilised for the erection of shelters. One of these bastions is opposite the Bath Hotel.

The double set of steps leading to the promenade from the cliff-top, near the Hotel Metropole, has been abolished, and a more convenient single set made in their place. The steps to the beach on the easternmost side of the pier have also been replaced by a concreted slope, in the opposite direction to what the steps were. Tar and limestone paving is being laid the whole length of the promenade.

In the centre of the eastern section are well-appointed lavatories, with handsome red-brick exteriors.

At a point equidistant from the eastern and western ends of the promenade a spacious bastion leads to the entrance of a handsome pier. The central approach is by a broad flight of steps. On either side are wide slopes of easy gradient, surmounted by iron railings. At the entrance to the pier are two imposing ornamental iron gates, the work of Messrs. Macfarlane, of Glasgow.

To right and left of these are turnstiles and gracefully designed kiosks. On the pillars adjoining the entrance, and facing the pier approach is inscribed "C.P.C. 1900." Mr. Alfred Thorne, of Westminster, is the contractor for the pier, which is about half completed.

When finished it will be 500 feet in length, with a splendid head 140 feet long and 110 feet wide. About 240 feet is now open to the public. At the seaward end, and also at the entrance, the pier is 60 feet wide, 40 feet being its narrowest width.

It is constructed on iron columns, which support steel lattice girders. The flooring of the pier is of fir wood. Down the centre of the pier are iron standards, each supporting three lamps. The newest reflecting lanterns are used, fitted with very powerful incandescent lights. These are at frequent intervals, so that the pier will be exceptionally well lighted.

The seating accommodation is admirable and extremely comfortable. There are seats on either side of the pier, and a double row down the middle, with, of course, breaks for the convenience of visitors wishing to cross from one side to the other.

A handsome octagonal bandstand is placed at the end of the pier for the present season, but on the completion of the whole erection will be moved to the extensive pier-head.

Most comfortable chairs for the use of visitors face the bandstand.

During the season, commencing on Monday last, the Blue Viennese Band will here give two performances daily.

Near the bandstand, on either side of the Pier, are shelters, each with four bays facing seawards and four bays looking inwards.

The extension of the Pier will be proceeded with during the season, but it is not anticipated that any further portion will be opened to the public until next year.

Seats, kiosks, shelters, bandstand, gates, and balustrades on the Pier are all painted white.

The ceremony of opening the Pier was performed on Monday by Mr. A. E. Jarvis, chairman of the Protection Commissioners. Other members of the Board present were Messrs. J. Curtis, L. G. Burton, J. W. Jefferson, A. C. Savin, J. Bower, H. Rust, G. M. Bultitude, J. Riches, R. A. Clarke, J. Riches, jun., T. Puxley, W. Churchyard, J. Lovelace, Ambrose Burton, and E. M. Hansell (Clerk). Mr. J. K. Frost (Clerk of the District Council), Mr. A. Thorne (the contractor), and Mr. Douglass (the engineer), were also present.

The proceedings were very brief. Mr. Jarvis, in formally declaring the Pier open, expressed the hope that all were satisfied with the work carried out. Though not able to open a longer portion this year he congratulated them that they had now some 7,000 more square feet than on the old jetty. By next season they would have the whole completed.

He hoped the pier would be the means of increasing the number of visitors to Cromer and of providing a lasting benefit to the place (Cheers). He also expressed the opinion that the sea front of Cromer was second to none in England.

THE CONSTRUCTION OF CROMER PIER

The turnstiles were then unlocked, the "No Admittance" board reversed, and the pier perambulated. Before closing time 1,650 persons had passed through the turnstiles.

The western section of the work, for which the contractors are Messrs. B. Cooke and Co., London, is far from complete. When finished it will be similar to the eastern section, having concrete sea wall, semi-circular bastions, slopes to the beach, &c.

There will also be a lavatory for both sexes, and a double concreted slope from the cliff-top. The face of the cliffs has been neatly sloped and levelled, and considerable improvement effected in many ways. There is also a large shelter erected last year.

A slope near this has been considerably lengthened, thus reducing the gradient.

This part of the promenade, when complete, will extend westwards past the Grand Hotel, and will be 1,760 feet in length.

Along the whole length of the sea-front there have been very extensive additions to the lighting, which is by incandescent gas. The contract for this was placed with Messrs. Lewellen and Co., of Clacton-on-Sea. The paving contract was shared by Messrs. Constable and Co. and the Victoria Stone Company, London.

This mile long promenade is thus seen to be well-paved, well-lighted, and well-seated, and is bound to add greatly to Cromer's prestige as one of the most progressive watering places in England. The total cost of sea-front improvements will involve an outlay of £50,000, of which £30,000 has already been expended.

The engineers for the whole improvement scheme are Messrs. Douglass and Arnott, Westminster.

THE CONSTRUCTION OF CROMER PIER

*Norfolk Museums Service, Cromer Museum, CRRMU : CP6467
East promenade (early 20th century)*

Eastern Daily Press: Saturday 21st July 1900

Cromer – The opening of the pier has given a splendid send off to the season.

The pier and promenades now present a very animated appearance each day. Especially is this so in the evenings, when the great improvements made on the sea front is the more noticeable.

The illuminated promenades and attractive pier are then at their best. The Blue Viennese Band is very popular, and large numbers attend the morning and evening performances. Boating is also much more in evidence, and many of the lighter craft are to be seen near the Pier when the band plays. Over 3,000 persons passed the turnstiles by Tuesday night. The excellent manner in which the Pier is fitted up calls forth most favourable comments from visitors.

Eastern Daily Press: Tuesday 24th July 1900

CROMER PIER
A RESERVED ENCLOSURE

A special meeting of the Cromer Protection Commissioners was held yesterday at the Clerk's Office, Church Street, Cromer, Mr. A. E. Jarvis in the chair. There were present Messrs. J. Curtis, R. A. Clarke, J. Smith, J. Lovelace, A. C. Savin, G. Riches, A. Burton, T. Puxley, J. Riches, jun., and L. G. Burton.

The Chairman said the meeting was called to consider a proposal made to enclose a small space on the Pier just round the bandstand for providing reserved seats. He had received several complaints from visitors in the habit of going down after dinner and unable to find seats.

The best seats were taken before the band commenced playing, and were not vacated until the evening's performance was over. It was thought that by reserving a few seats at a small extra charge of 2d. satisfaction would be given to everyone.

Mr. R. A. Clarke felt that if anything there was too much seating accommodation, and not sufficient space for promenading. Mr. J. Riches, jun., could not support the scheme with the limited space they at present had on the Pier.

Mr. Curtis was of opinion a space should be reserved. Mr. T. Puxley thought the proposal would meet with much objection. Mr. Lovelace said he had seen the first seats filled with children, and when visitors came down there were none for them.

The Chairman said they had written to the Board of Trade on the subject. In reply the Department said it was not for them to express an opinion on the matter.

The seating accommodation on the Pier was over 500. He was down on Saturday night, when every seat was filled. Mr. G. Riches thought no extra charge should be made until more seating accommodation was provided. He did not believe in sacrificing the promenades for the benefit of the Pier.

Mr. Savin was of the same opinion. He also thought there were many persons who would not go on the Pier even if it were free. Mr. Smith proposed the making of a reserved space on the Pier at an additional charge of twopence a seat. Mr. Lovelace seconded. Mr. T. Puxley moved, as an amendment, that no alteration be made this year. Mr. Clarke seconded.

The Chairman said he had received a letter from Mr. F. W. Rogers in favour of the proposal. On a division 5 voted for the amendment and 6 against. The motion was then put to the meeting, and carried.

The Morning Leader (London): Tuesday 31st July 1900

Cromer – Brilliant weather continues and the town is fast filling up with visitors. On Thursday the Baconsthorpe and district flower show is held in the grounds of Cromer Hall.

Next week cycling and athletic sports take place in Sheringham park. In addition to playing mornings and evenings on week days the Blue Viennese Band also performs on the pier on Sunday evenings after church hours.

The Sketch: Wednesday 1st August 1900

THE OPENING OF THE NEW PIER AT CROMER: VISITORS WAITING FOR THE COMMISSIONERS TO DECLARE IT OPEN.

The Suffolk and Essex Free Press: Wednesday Evening 1st August 1900

Cromer, that interesting pleasure resort on the East Coast, the centre of "Poppyland," is being modernised. A new pier was opened recently, and when completed will have cost £12,000.

Those who remember the quaint old jetty, on which the lights were turned out at nine even in the height of the season, will heave a sigh of regret at this news. Will the town now become the centre of cheap steamboat trips?

Pall Mall Gazette: Friday 3rd August 1900

Sunday Music on Cromer Pier

Since the opening of Cromer Pier, the band has played thereon every Sunday evening. A petition, signed by local owners of property, has been presented to the Protection Commissioners, the local authority, deprecating the innovation both on religious and financial grounds.

The Commissioners, however, have decided to continue Sunday performances, but to have sacred music only.

The Downham Market Gazette: Saturday 11th August 1900

Cromer felt the full force of the storm, *(possibly Friday, 3rd August, 1900)* and the gale making from the north-west, big seas were running. Crowds watched the magnificent spectacle on the sea front.

Beyond the wrecking of the pile staging at the end of the Pier and a few lamps broken on the Pier, no great damage was done.

THE CONSTRUCTION OF CROMER PIER

*Norfolk Museums Service, Cromer Museum, CRRMU : 2011.31.12
Crowds on the pier with the broken lamps visible*

Eastern Evening News: Thursday 6th September 1900

A general meeting was held yesterday at the Clerk's Office, Church Street, Cromer, Mr. A. E. Jarvis in the chair. There were present Messrs. J. Curtis, R. A. Clarke, J. Riches, jun., J. Lovelace, H. Rust, J. Bower, T. Puxley, J. Riches, sen., A. Burton, and A. C. Savin. Mr. Douglass (Messrs. Douglass & Arnott) also attended.

The Clerk reported a credit balance at the bank of £1,252 14s. 6d. on the general account, and £356 3s. 3d. on the loan account. Also, that since the last statement £246 3s. 5d. had been collected in rates.

The following payments were approved: – Board of Trade (per Mr. McArthur) inspecting pier, £2 2s.; W. Pilkington, superintendent of works, four weeks' salary, £15 15s.; Pier and Parade wages, five weeks,

£27 9s. 5d.; R. Allen, wage payments, five weeks, £52 18s. 3d.; and Keith, Prowse, & Co., services of band from 27th July to 2nd September, five weeks, £56 – £280.

The Works Committee recommended that Mr. Weatherall be appointed clerk of the works at a salary of £2 2s. a week. This, on the motion of Mr. Curtis, seconded by Mr. Clarke, was agreed to.

Some discussion arose with respect to the use of the Promenade by the lifeboat.

The Lifeboat Institution had asked leave to take their boat along the Promenade.

The Works Committee recommended the refusal of the request, pointing out that there was now a better and wider slipway for launching than hitherto.

Mr. J. Riches, jun., thought the question of saving life was of more importance than damage to lamp posts on the Promenade.

The Chairman – Which was the quickest, to go along the Promenade with the Cromer boat or for the lifeboat to come from Sheringham.

Mr. J. Riches, sen., understood the Promenade was widened opposite Beach House in order to allow of the lifeboat going along.

Mr. T. Puxley was strongly of opinion that the lifeboat should have the privilege of using the Promenade in case of urgency. To talk of the Sheringham lifeboat coming to the rescue of a wreck opposite the town before the Cromer boat reached it was simply absurd.

The Chairman – What in the event of damage done to the Promenade?

Mr. Puxley – The institution would have to pay.

Mr. Rust – The engineer said it was hardly safe to take that weight.

Mr. Puxley thought it a great pity no slipway was provided on the Western Promenade.

The engineer said there was one at the far end.

Mr. J. Riches, jun., held there should be one opposite the Grand Hotel. Was it not a fact that on the plan one was shown there? Also, that it was knocked out because the Lifeboat Institution would not meet them with regard to the east gangway slipway.

He asked the Chairman if he did not recall a conversation about this he had with him on the Cliff.

The Chairman had no recollection. Some people had a very fertile imagination.

The committee's recommendation was on the advice of their engineer.

Mr. Douglass said that according to instructions the Promenades were tar paved to meet the requirements of light traffic, such as bath chairs.

The lifeboat and carriages would weigh about 7 tons. The Promenade was wide enough for the lifeboat, but it would leave marks where it had passed over.

Mr. Rust proposed the adoption of the committee's recommendation refusing sanction. – Mr. Bower seconded.

Mr. Puxley moved an amendment that leave be granted in case of emergency, the lifeboat authorities to make good any damage. – Mr. J. Riches, jun., seconded. The amendment was lost by one vote, five voting for and six against.

The application of the Blue Viennese Band for a benefit performance on Thursday, 13th September, was granted.

The engagement of the band ceases on the 17th September, and a request that they be allowed to play on the Pier up to the 20th and pay the Commissioners 20 per cent. of the takings of those four extra days was also granted.

The Chairman said the total receipts from the Pier were £595 6s. 6d. That paid for band and wages, and he thought the result very satisfactory.

Bills to the total of £12 15s. 9d. were ordered to be paid. The following payments were also authorised: – Messrs. Douglass & Arnott (commission), £108 7s. 9d.; and Messrs. B. Cooke & Co., on account western works, £1,000; also to the Royal London Friendly Society £380 16s., being the amount of principle and interest, less income tax, due on 28th September, with respect to the loan of £7,000.

(Please note the benefit concert appears to have been held on Thursday, 20th September, 1900).

The Morning Leader (London): Friday 14th September 1900

CROMER

Bright and genial weather prevails, and as yet there seems to be no appreciable falling off in the number of visitors. The Blue Viennese Band have a benefit concert on the pier on Thursday. Next week they will come to the end of their season engagement. The Town Hall amusements continue to draw good houses.

Given a continuance of fine weather visitors are not likely to thin out very much before the close of the month.

The Ealing Gazette and West Middlesex Observer
"The Gazette": Saturday 15th September 1900

"THREE SISTERS BY THE SEA."
By Clement Scott

Scarcely fourteen years ago, a simple and primitive little hamlet, with a Lighthouse, and a fine sea down, an East Anglian church hemmed in by the few diminutive shops that Cromer boasted, a rickety pier, on which nobody walked, very scant accommodation for travellers, little known to the great world of London, and only locally patronised as a bathing place, Cromer has become one of the most fashionable health resorts on the East Coast of England.

Norfolk Museums Service, Cromer Museum, CRRMU : 2011.31.10
Pier forecourt

Downham Market Gazette: Saturday 22nd September 1900

PIER BAND BENEFIT. – The benefit concert given by the Blue Viennese Band on the Pier on Thursday evening was very successful, the Pier being thronged with an enthusiastic audience, who thoroughly appreciated the programme, which was as follows: -

March – "Soldier's Life" (Schmeling)
Valse – "Engaged" (Waldteufel)
Overture – "Semiramis" (Rossini)
Song – "The Holy City" by Moffat Ford
"The Turkish Patrol" (Michaelis)
Selection – "The Belle of New York" (Kerker)
Cornet solo – "Bolero varie"
"Toreador" (Ch. Le Thiere), by Mr. T. Clinton
"Second Rhapsody" (arranged by Marinari), (Liszt)
Overture – "William Tell" (Rossini)
Duet – "Love's Declaration" (Marinari), by Signor Marinari and Gallo*
Song – "Mary" (Richardson), by Mr. Moffat Ford
Valse – "Lustige Bruder" (Vollstedt)
Selection – "San Toy" (Jones)
Galop – "The Railway Train" (Gille)*

Unclear print on original source

Eastern Evening News: Saturday 22nd September 1900

Cromer – On Thursday, the Blue Viennese Band gave the last of their season's performances.

The event attracted a large crowd on the Pier. At the close of the programme "Auld Lang Syne" was introduced as a final touch to an interesting scene. Since the Pier was opened on July 16th, over 80,000 persons have passed the turnstiles. This satisfactory result says much for the popularity of an excellent band and the splendid musical performances given during the season months.

The Norfolk News: Saturday 6th October 1900

A meeting was held on Wednesday at the Clerk's Office, Church Street, Cromer, Mr. A. E. Jarvis in the chair.

The Deputy Clerk reported the following credit balances at the bank: – General account £1,288 11s. 11d., and loan account £1,232 6s. 9d.

He also reported that during the month rates to the amount of £252 4s. 4d. had been collected. On the motion of Mr. Curtis, seconded by Mr. Clarke, various payments were sanctioned.

They included £112 to Messrs. Keith, Prowse, & Co. for the last fortnight's engagement of the band. The Deputy-Clerk reported that the total Pier receipts from commencement to the end of September was £767 17s. 2d. The September receipts were £161. On the recommendation of the Works Committee the following payments were authorised: – Mr. A. Thorne, Pier (contractor), £1,748 8s. 9d.; McDowall, Steven & Co., bandstand, £374; Messrs. Douglass & Arnott, commission, £50.

The Works Committee reported that Mr. W. Kemp had asked leave for his band to play on the Pier on Thursday and Friday in each week, he to take cash proceeds, and hand over half to the Commissioners. It was decided to grant permission for October, Mr. Kemp to give notice if the performances are discontinued. It was also decided to have no enclosures on the Pier.

On the motion of Mr. Clarke, seconded by Mr. Curtis, it was resolved to communicate with Messrs. Keith, Prowse, & Co. with a view to securing a band for next season. Arising out of a letter received from the National Lifeboat Institution, Mr. J. Riches, jun., gave notice of motion to rescind the resolution passed at the last meeting relative to the use of the promenade by the lifeboat in case of emergency.

The seal of the Board was authorised to be affixed to the mortgage for securing £43,500, repayment to extend over a period of sixty years in equal half-yearly instalments, principal and interest, of £959 1s. 11d. each year. On the motion of Mr. G. Riches, seconded by Mr. Curtis, Mr. Edward Gurney Buxton was appointed treasurer to the Board.

Norwich Mercury: Saturday 10th November 1900

Mr. A. E. Jarvis presided over a meeting of the Commissioners on Wednesday. The Clerk reported the following credit balances in bank pass book: – General account £932 18s. 1d., and loan account £481 0s. 9d. The collector's statement for the month show receipts of £323 8s. 9d. Wage payments by R. Allen to the amount of £28 6s. 3d. were confirmed.

THE CONSTRUCTION OF CROMER PIER

The Pier receipts from September 30th to November 4th were £7 19s. 4d. The Works Committee gave a detailed report of the winter alterations with respect to the staff employed and the lighting on the sea front during the winter months. It was decided to employ W. H. Neal in his position on the pier at a wage of 8s. per week, keeping the Pier open from 9.30 a.m. to 4 p.m., and extra payment for additional hours.

The same committee recommended the acceptance of (A) the tender of Messrs. English Bros. for the supply of timber required for extension of Doctor's Steps groyne, and (B) that of Messrs. John Turner and Co. for supplying pile shoes and spikes.

As a result of the engineer's report, they also recommended that the two worst cracks in the wall of the zig-zag approach to the Promenade be repaired as suggested, that the tar paving be renewed where necessary, and that a buttress be constructed near the old band stand.

The committee further recommended the payment of the following sums: – Messrs. B. Cooke and Co., western section £876 7s. 3d.; Mr. A. Thorne (Pier substructure), £791 8s. 6d.; ditto superstructure, £159 10s. 8d.; Messrs. Douglass and Arnott, engineers, commission, £104 5s. 5d. The report was adopted. Mr. A. Thorne's tender of £1,135 for the Pierhead shelter, to be completed by the end of April, was accepted.

The Clerk reported that the net cost of gas used for the quarter ending September 30th was £23 7s. 1d. This included the Pier and the lighting of all the Commissioners' works. The payment of this and some minor accounts were authorised.

The Works Committee submitted a scheme for the improvement of the Marrams at an estimated cost of £1,443 6s. 10d. This gave rise to a little discussion. Mr. Curtis thought it would be wise to wait for a time.

Mr. Douglass (the engineer) said it would be cheaper to do the work now than later.

It would have to be done at some time. Mr. J. Riches, jun., asked if the proposed expenditure would overstep the limit of £45,000 allowed them by the Act, or would they have to go to the Board of Trade for more? The Clerk believed the balance they had would suffice for the work.

The scheme, with a slight alteration as to the length of a proposed wall, was then adopted. This wall will extend 270 feet from the east end of the Marrams.

According to notice given, Mr. J. Riches, jun., proposed the rescinding of a resolution passed on 5th September, prohibiting the lifeboat from using the Promenade. Mr. Burton seconded, and this was agreed to. Mr. Riches then moved that permission be given the National Lifeboat Institution to take their boat along the Promenade, on condition they make good any damage caused, also that as requested by the institution a slipway be erected near the Grand Hotel. Mr. Curtis seconded, and this was carried.

The Clerk reported that correspondence had passed between him and Messrs. Keith, Prowse, and Co., of London, with regard to securing a band for next season.

The firm's offer was considered, and on the motion of the Chairman, seconded by Mr. Curtis, it was decided to make a counter offer of a nine weeks' engagement of twelve performers and conductor at £56 per week from July 5th to September 5th.

Also, on their coming down for Whitsuntide they take all receipts up to July 5th, and after September 5th to end of that month on paying the Board 17 ½ per cent.

The Band also to have permission to have Saturday afternoon concerts outside the season engagement, and pay the Board 17 ½ per cent. on takings. Also, if desired, to have vocalists on Sunday evenings out of season, but that during the nine weeks' engagement none to be allowed, and only sacred music performed.

Eastern Evening News:
Thursday 6th December 1900 (incomplete)

A meeting was held yesterday at the Clerk's Office, Church Street, Cromer, Mr. A. E. Jarvis in the chair. There were present Messrs. J. Curtis, J. W. Jefferson, W. Churchyard, A. C. Savin, J. Bower, F. W. Rogers, T. Puxley, G. M. Bultitude, J. Riches, jun., R. A. Clarke, and J. Riches, sen. Messrs. Douglass & Arnott, engineers, also attended.

The Clerk reported that the following credit balance stood in the bank passbooks, general account £1,318 19s. 4d., and loan ditto £555 4s. 5d.

The collector's statement showed that rates to the amount of £371 10s. 5d. had been got in since the last meeting. Various wage payments were confirmed, also one of £9 7s. 3d. for insurance of the Board's workmen, as last year.

The Clerk reported that, in granting the Lifeboat Institution leave to take their boat along the Promenade, the institution had written accepting full liability for any damage that may be done.

The Works Committee reported that a plan for the proposed slipway on the Western Promenade had been submitted to them, but they recommended that prior to its being carried out the Lifeboat Institution should test the possibility of taking their boat up the steps leading from the east gangway on to the Promenade.

The committee also reported that Messrs. Keith, Prowse, & Co. accepted the Board's terms for next season's band on one condition.

And this, permission to have Saturday afternoon concerts on the Pier throughout the season, they recommended should be granted. The committee further recommended the acceptance of the only tender received for work on the Marrams.

This was Messrs. Cooke & Co.'s for £894. On the motion of Mr. Churchyard, seconded by Mr. Savin, the report of the committee was adopted. Mr. Savin proposed, and Mr. Bower seconded, the payment of the following sums: – Insurance of Pier against fire to 16th April, £3 15s. Messrs. Girling & Smith, fittings, 12s. 6d.

And as certified by the engineers – Messrs. Fasey & Son, eastern section contractors, £413 7s. 9d.; Messrs. Cooke & Co., western section, £475 13s. 10d., and Messrs. Douglass & Arnott, engineers' commission, £83 10s. 9d.

The Clerk read a letter from Mr. J. Davies requesting permission to stand his bathing machines on the West Promenade on a payment of 2s. each per year. Mr. Savin was against the idea being entertained.

The machines were bad for the Promenade, and he also thought that to grant leave would set a bad precedent. He proposed the refusal of the application. Mr. Rogers seconded, and it was agreed to.

Some discussion ensued with respect to the narrowing of the Western Promenade at the Runton end.

The original plan showed a uniform width of 40 ft., but a portion of it has been constructed only 20 ft. wide. Mr. Bultitude asked if it was possible to get the extra width. Mr. Douglass (the engineer) said it was a matter of cutting into the cliff.

The deviation was made subsequent to and as the result of the landslip. Mr. J. Riches thought the fact was that the wall had been carried too near the cliff. Mr. T. Puxley considered no money or pains should be spared to carry out the original plan.

The Chairman said as he understood the case it was this. If they wanted a 40 ft. promenade width they would have to take a lot of the cliff down and pay for it. If left alone it would come down in a matter of time.

They would then get the width and save the cost. Mr. Douglass said that was so. The work was simply a matter of finance. Fifty to sixty tonnes of stuff would have to be excavated to get the 40 ft. width. Mr. Puxley complained that as a Commissioner, he was not informed of the alteration at the time of the landslip.

Mr. Douglass said the landslip took place early in the year, and he had reported on it.

(The rest of the article is incomplete; however, the Commissioners requested the engineers to produce plans and estimates for the widening of the western promenade to 40 feet).

Norfolk Museums Service, Cromer Museum, CRRMU : CP6946
The Hotel de Paris from the pier

Chapter Five – 1901

Eastern Daily Press: Thursday 3rd January 1901

A general meeting was held yesterday at the Clerk's Office, Church Street, Cromer, Mr. J. Lovelace in the chair. There were present Messrs. J. Curtis, R. A. Clarke, H. Rust, J. Riches, jun., G. M. Bultitude, A. Burton, A. C. Savin, F. W. Rogers, J. W. Jefferson, T. Puxley, and L. G. Burton. Mr. Arnott (Messrs. Douglass & Arnott) also attended.

The Clerk reported the following credit balance in the bank pass books: – General account £1,402 0s. 7d., and loan account £87 8s. 11d. On the motion of Mr. Curtis, seconded by Mr. Clarke it was resolved to transfer the sum of £1,700 from the deposit to the loan account.

The collector's statement for the month showed rates to the amount of £102 14s. 9d. received. On the motion of Mr. Clarke, seconded by Mr. Savin, the following payments were confirmed, viz., Mr. Weatherall, clerk of works, salary for month, £8 8s.; and R. Allen, wage payments, £22 14s. 3d.

The Works Committee reported that the Royal National Lifeboat Institution had written asking that the slipway across the eastern groyne should be at least 20 ft. wide, and of sufficient strength to bear the lifeboat on her carriage. It was recommended that the institution should be informed that a slipway of timber had been completed to a width of 12 ft., and that it would not be possible to extend it to 20 ft. and make it sufficiently strong to bear the lifeboat on its carriage without necessitating alterations in the construction. At the same time they took the opportunity to point out that they understood that, if necessary, the lifeboat would be safely taken over the present slipway minus the carriage.

The committee also recommended the taking of legal proceedings against bathing-machine owners for obstructing the promenade with their machines.

They further recommended payments be made as follows: – Income-tax £12 2s., Mr. A. Fox (chairs) £3 11s. 3d., Messrs. English Bros. (timber) £40 11s. 7d., Mr. John Turner (spikes and pile shoes) £3 18s. 2d., and

Messrs. A. Fasey & Son (eastern section of promenade) £350, and Mr. A. Thorne (Pier) £691 3s., as certified by the engineers.

The Clerk said the six months for the completion of Messrs. Fasey's contract had now expired. The sum of £350 was a portion of the 10 per cent. retention money held up to now by the Board. The payment of £52 8s. 7d. to the engineers, their commission on previous certificates, was also recommended by the committee. On the motion of Mr. Rogers, seconded by Mr. Rust, the report was adopted.

The Clerk having read a circular letter, under date 12th December, from Messrs. W. H. Tilston & Son as to pier insurance, he was instructed to attend the adjourned meeting to be held on 15th January, and the Board favoured (1) that a strong representation should in the first instance be made to the existing insurance organisations with a view to insurance in the ordinary way of several piers together; (2) that, failing this, the Clerk should report to the meeting that the Commissioners would be willing to join a mutual indemnity association upon being satisfied that the terms upon which it may be formed were equitable and the basis sound, and also that a considerable number of pier authorities come to a similar conclusion, and (3) that the Clerk be instructed to pay a sum not exceeding three guineas towards the expenses of Messrs. Tilston & Son in the event of any insurance scheme failing to be carried through, provided that at least ten other representatives agree to the same course.

A plan for the repair of the zig-zag approach to the promenade was submitted by the engineers. It was approved, and it was decided to invite tenders for the work, to be in by next meeting. The engineers also submitted a plan and estimate for widening the western promenade, the subject of discussion at the December meeting of the Board. The cost was placed at £1,500.

Before coming to a decision on the matter it was resolved that the engineers should present an alternative scheme, whereby the uniform width of 40 ft. could be had by carrying the wall seaward from a point near the extreme western bastion of the existing Promenade.

Eastern Daily Press: Thursday 7th February 1901

A meeting was held yesterday at the Clerk's Office, Church Street, Cromer, Mr. A. E. Jarvis in the chair. Messrs. Douglass & Arnott, the engineers, also attended.

The Clerk reported the following credit balances in the bank pass books, viz: – General account £1,389 19s. 2d., and loan ditto £110 12s. 6d. During the month rates to the amount of £46 15s. 5d. had been collected.

The Clerk was instructed to take legal proceedings for the recovery of rates where necessary. The payment of ten guineas to Mr. Weatherall, four weeks' salary as clerk of the works, and wage payments by R. Allen to the total of £23 13s. 6d. were confirmed. The Board also authorised the transfer of £1,250 from deposit to loan account.

The engineers reported that since last month eleven wrought iron piles had been driven in the pier-head, leaving only three more to complete the pile driving.

They also stated that practically the whole of the steel and iron work to finish the pier had been delivered. The wood work of the pier-head shelter was ready for delivery.

An average of twenty-two men had found employment on the work. As regards the Marrams improvement from ten to twelve men had been engaged, and two-thirds of the work was done.

The Works Committee reported that the engineer, as instructed, had submitted a plan for the proposed widening of the Runton end of the Western Parade to secure a uniform width of 40 ft. The estimated cost was £2,160. The scheme suggested the taking of a new wall seaward from a point near where the Parade now begins to narrow.

The engineers state that "the wall would be similar in construction to that already built, and will be erected 17 feet in advance of the latter, thus giving a total clear width of 40 feet. The junction between the position of the parade, now 40 feet in width, and the new work would be affected by the construction of a bold sweep of wall worked by a bastion. A second bastion might be constructed in front of the existing west bastion, where also a flight of steps, similar to those proposed at the Grand Hotel bastion, could be placed."

The committee recommended that the consideration of the subject be postponed.

Mr. Lovelace moved the adoption of the committee. He thought they should first get the opinion of the ratepayers before spending so much money. Mr. R. A. Clarke seconded. The Chairman said the subject would not be discussed until a previous resolution of the Board had been rescinded. The committee's recommendation was agreed to. Mr. J. Riches, jun., then gave notice of rescinding the motion.

The Works Committee reported that Messrs. B. Cooke & Co.'s tender of £688 was the only one received for the work on the zig-zag approach, and recommended acceptance of same.

The committee also stated that the Royal National Lifeboat Institution had written with respect to the "satisfactory" trial passage of the lifeboat along the promenade.

The institution suggested that certain lamp posts should be altered, one near the east gangway slip and the other near the proposed Grand Hotel slipway.

Also, that at the former one and at the latter two posts be fixed for the use of the lifeboat. The committee recommended that the institution be informed (1) of the extent and cost of the damage done by the lifeboat's passage, (2) that they were willing to have moveable posts, subject to position having their approval, but (3) declining to grant request for removal of the lamp posts.

The same committee recommended the following payments as certified by the engineers: – Mr. A. Thorne on account of pier £764 9s. 6d., Messrs. B. Cooke & Co., ditto Marrams, £531, Messrs. Douglass & Arnott, commission on previous certificates, £52 1s. 2d. Payment of small bills to the amount of £9 13s. 2d. was also recommended.

On the motion of Mr. Savin, seconded by Mr. Churchyard, the various recommendations of the committee were adopted.

Last year's committee to inspect and settle register of electors was appointed on the motion of Mr. Bower, seconded by Mr. A. Burton.

The Clerk stated that this year's retiring members of the Board were Messrs. F. W. Rogers, J. Curtis, W. Churchyard, L. G. Burton and J. Riches, jun. The election would be in May.

Mr. J. Riches, jun., proposed that specifications be prepared and tenders invited for the construction of the Grand Hotel slipway. Mr. Curtis seconded. Mr. Rogers moved an amendment that the subject be postponed until the Board had a reply from the Royal National Lifeboat Institution to the letter they had resolved to send.

He thought as the institution had so much to say in the matter, they should know what they were prepared to do. Mr. Bower seconded, and the amendment was carried by 8 to 5. Mr. Lovelace thought they had no further need for the services of the Clerk of the Works.

In his opinion, R. Allen was quite able to do all that was now required. He therefore proposed that Mr. Weatherall's engagement be terminated. Mr. J. Riches, jun., seconded.

Mr. Douglass said the Board were spending money at the rate of about £1,200 to £1,400 a month. There was enough work to continue the Clerk of the Works' services until Easter.

The cost of keeping him would be less than 1 per cent. on the money expended. Mr. F. W. Rogers said he brought up the question at the Works Committee that morning thinking they might dispense with the Clerk of the Works.

But after hearing the explanation of the engineer he thought the Board might retain him until Easter in view of the new work to be carried out. He, therefore, moved an amendment that Mr. Weatherall's services be retained until Easter.

Mr. Churchyard seconded. On a vote 5 were for and 6 against the amendment, and on being put to the meeting as a substantive motion the resolution was carried by one. Two members did not vote.

Eastern Daily Press: Friday 15th February 1901

Yesterday, at the Town Hall, Cromer, a Local Government Board inquiry was held into the application of the Urban District Council for sanction to borrow £500 for works of surface water drainage. There was no opposition, and the proceedings were over in about ten minutes.

Mr. A. F. Scott (Surveyor) and Mr. J. Verry, in the absence through indisposition of Mr. J. K. Frost (Clerk) represented the Council. The only members present were Mr. F. W. Rogers and Mr. J. Curtis. Mr. Verry stated that the rateable value of the town was £33,739 17s. 6d., and the assessable £32,233 0s. 10d.

The population in 1891, excluding Suffield Park, was 2,197, and in 1900, inclusive of that area, estimated at 3,825. There were 850 inhabited houses, and the total area of the urban district 938 acres.

There were outstanding loans to the amount of £24,603 19s. The loan now asked was for the purpose of carrying out works of surface water drainage in the Runton Road, with an outfall discharge to the Beach.

Up to the present time there has been no separate surface water system of sewerage in force in Cromer. But in passing plans for new roads which have recently been submitted, the Council have required surface water drains to be laid with an outfall discharge into the existing watercourses.

Plans for new roads on the land adjoining Runton Road, which forms part of the Cromer Hall building estate, have recently been submitted to the Council.

In passing them the Council stipulated that separate surface water sewers should be laid in each street.

To deal with this surface water the Council proposed to lay the present sewer, which will run from the highest point on the Runton Road to a point opposite Beach Road, at which place it will return and run down the face of the Cliff to the Beach. The sewerage of the town passes through septic tanks, which have recently been constructed.

As it is desirable that as much of the surface water as possible should be excluded from these tanks, it is proposed to construct the outfall.

The Cromer Protection Commissioners, under whose works the outfall will have to pass, have signified their approval and given their consent to the work being carried out subject to it being completed by the end of March. The loan was asked for thirty years. Mr. Scott then gave details of the work.

The Norfolk News (Second Sheet): Saturday 9th March 1901

A meeting was held on Wednesday, at the Clerk's Office, Church Street, Cromer, Mr. A. E. Jarvis in the chair. There were present Messrs. R. A. Clarke, J. Curtis, J. Bower, A. Burton, J. Riches, jun., A. C. Savin, G. Riches, J. W. Jefferson, and T. Puxley.

Mr. Arnott (Messrs. Douglass & Arnott, engineers), also attended the meeting.

The Clerk reported the following credit balance in bank pass books, viz: – General account £422 3s. 11d., and loan ditto £30 18s. 5d. The collector's statement showed rates collected during the month £46 9s. 11d. R. Allen's report was received, and wage payments by him to the amount of £18 16s. 3d. were confirmed.

The Works Committee reported as to the foundations of the zig-zag approach bastion. Mr. Arnott presented a statement showing the necessity for going down a further 6 ft., or 9 ft. in all, from promenade level to get a firm foundation for the bastion and the flank walls on either side. He added there was no alternative course, and the estimated cost was £200.

The committee, as a matter of urgency, had authorised the bastion foundation, which was about half the total cost, or some £116.

Mr. J. Riches, jun., complained that the committee had authorised expenditure on their own responsibility. He thought a special meeting of the Board should have been called.

The Chairman said what the committee did they did within the powers given them in the Act.

By that twenty-four hours notice was required to call a special meeting, and the urgency of the bastion work did not permit of so long a delay.

Mr. Savin failed to see that the Board could have done other than the committee, even had they been consulted. On the motion of Mr. Curtis, seconded by Mr. Burton, the committee's action was approved. On the motion of Mr. Curtis, seconded by Mr. Savin, the further outlay with regard to the flank walls was authorised.

The engineer reported that the last of the wrought iron piles for the Pier was driven in on February 9th, and that the contractor had now removed his engines, blacksmith's and other shops.

He also reported as to the progress made with the Marrams improvement. Mr. G. Riches called attention to the present condition of the cliff slopes, which were disgraceful. He felt it would be far better to make a good retaining wall and reduce the slope of the cliff at once than spend money on the Beach by widening the Promenade. In making the sea wall as they did, he thought the engineers were quite right.

And instead of spending £2,000 on extending the Promenade seaward, the Board should spend £300 on sloping the cliff and raising the height of the retaining wall.

He proposed that the engineers prepare plans in accordance with the suggestion.

Mr. J. Riches, jun., seconded, and this was agreed to.

The following payments were authorised: – Messrs. B. Cooke & Co., £200, in respect to Marrams improvement; Messrs. Douglass & Arnott, engineers, commission on previous certificates, £64 15s. 6d.; and Mr. A. Thorne, pier contractor, on account, £100. This last was subject to the Works Committee being satisfied as to certain extra items.

The Clerk read a letter from the National Lifeboat Institution, in which they agreed to pay £26, the extent of damage done to the Promenade by the passage of the lifeboat. They, however, thought it was rather a large sum, and hoped it might not be so costly after all.

They also agreed to the terms as to the erection of the three posts on the Promenade, but regretted the Commissioners were unable to agree to the proposed alterations of the lamp posts. As regards the Grand Hotel slipway, the institution offered, in answer to the Board's inquiry, to contribute the sum of £25.

On the motion of Mr. J. Riches, jun., seconded by Mr. T. Puxley, it was resolved that in the event of compensation not being settled forthwith the Clerk should take the necessary steps to enable the Commissioners to take possession of that portion of the foreshore included in Lord Suffield's manor. The Clerk stated that the Board had already obtained possession of the falls and foreshore of which the Bond-Cabbell Trustees were the lords of the manor.

During the meeting a letter was read from the Urban District Council, who at present lease the foreshore from Lord Suffield, and that lease expires on 25th March. The question of whether on obtaining the foreshore from Lord Suffield the Commissioners should lease it to the Council or retain it under their own control was left over for a future date.

The resignation of Mr. Barclay of Hanworth Hall as a Commissioner, by reason of inability to attend the meetings, was on the motion of Mr. Curtis, seconded by Mr. J. Riches, jun., accepted with much regret.

Eastern Evening News: Monday 18th March 1901

CROMER

Early yesterday morning a steamer had a very narrow escape of coming ashore, if not of colliding with the Promenade Pier. The night was very foggy, and about one o' clock the coastguard on duty noticed what appeared to be the lights of a steamer coming straight on for the pier-head. At the very same moment the fog suddenly lifted, and this, with a flash from the Lighthouse light, evidently showed those aboard their danger, for in an instant the vessel's light told that the course was altered, and very soon she put out to sea in a southerly direction, blowing her siren now and again. The tide was about half-flow.

The Diss Express, and Norfolk and Suffolk Journal: Friday 22nd March 1901

A Norwegian vessel, named the Esras, of 266 tons register, bound from Kristiansand, ran ashore on the Hasbro' sands on Wednesday night at about eight o'clock.

On Thursday morning she was stranded on the Norfolk coast about opposite East Runton. Her position was one of peril to the crew, and just before 6 o'clock the Cromer and Sheringham Rocket Brigade were summoned. They however, found the Esras about a mile from shore, and were unable to render any assistance to the crew.

The Cromer lifeboat was also held in readiness, but she was unable to affect a launch. The vessel lay at the mercy of huge breakers, and eventually came broadside on the Runton beach, some 500 yards from land.

The rocket apparatus was got to work, but at first it failed. At the fifth attempt the Cromer "rocket" succeeded in reaching the Esras, and soon all was excitement. The first of the crew to enter the breeches was the cabin boy, and lashed by the waves he was successfully landed.

Time after time the performance was repeated, until only the mate was left on board. When his turn came, he soon entered the breeches, and after a rough journey had joined his comrades. All were cared for at the Lifeboat Inn, where they were taken by Sir T. Fowell Buxton, but later Captain Kennedy, of the Shipwrecked Mariners' Society, had the crew conveyed to Cromer.

*Norfolk Museums Service, Cromer Museum, CRRMU : 1981.80.1294
Cromer Lifeboat, east promenade*

Eastern Daily Press: Thursday 4th April 1901

CROMER PROTECTION
COMMISSIONERS

A meeting of this Board was held yesterday, at the Clerk's Office, Church Street, Cromer, Mr. A. E. Jarvis in the chair. There were present Messrs. J. Curtis, R. A. Clarke, H. Rust, J. Bower, G. Riches, F. W. Rogers, A. C. Savin, J. Riches, T. Puxley, J. Lovelace and W. Churchyard. Mr. Arnott (Messrs. Douglass & Arnott, the engineers), also attended.

On the motion of the Chairman, seconded by Mr. Rogers, a vote of condolence was passed with Mrs. J. Riches, sen., and family in the loss sustained by the death of Mr. James Riches, sen., for many years a Protection Commissioner.

The Clerk reported the following credit balance in the bank pass-books, viz., general account £458 4s. 1d., and loan ditto £139 15s. 5d. During the month rates to the amount of £5 10s. 7d. had been received by the Collector. There was still a sum of £57 1s. 3d. yet outstanding, and since the report was made this had been further reduced to about £53. Of that amount some £23 was made up of two items, viz., Postmaster General £10 3s. 9d., and Cromer Water Works Company £13 9s. 11d.

Some surprise was expressed that these were not yet paid. The Chairman said the rate was made out in June, and within two months the year would have expired. Mr. Rogers certainly thought the money should be got in. Mr. G. Riches also agreed that steps should be taken for its recovery.

The matter was left in the hands of the Clerk. The following payments were confirmed on the motion of Mr. Clarke, seconded by Mr. Savin: – R. Allen's wage payments for the month, £19 2s. 6d.: Alliance Insurance Company (loan), £915 11s. 11d.; Mr. Jarvis, £10 3s. 9d., excess of rate. The Board also authorised the transfer of the sum of £1,400 from loan to deposit account.

The engineers reported that the whole of the steel superstructure of the Pier was completed; the average number of men employed had been 25. Messrs. Cooke & Co. had been instructed to make good the damage done to the Promenade by the passage of the lifeboat. The previous damage done had been repaired.

The whole of the work on the Marrams was completed, with the exception of a few coping-stone and the erection of standards and railings.

They suggested that Messrs. Constable & Co. should recommence tar–paving after Easter. The report finished by noting progress had been made with the Hotel de Paris bastion.

Mr. Curtis asked the cost of damage done to the Promenade in the first instance by the lifeboat? Mr. Arnott – £26. Mr. Curtis said he could have got the work done for £5. Mr. J. Riches also thought the sum excessive. Mr. T. Puxley concurred. The Chairman replied that the representatives of the Lifeboat Institution were satisfied, and that being so, thought the matter might rest. The report was then adopted.

The Works Committee made various recommendations. The first was that Messrs. Cooke & Co.'s attention be called to the quality of "the grass" put on the Marrams.

The second was that three more hydrants be provided for the Pier, making six in all, and that arrangements be made with Cromer Water Works Company for connecting the pipes with the town main. Also, that alterations be made to the shelter seats on the Pier at a cost of £13 4s., and that from Saturday next the Pier be closed at 7 p.m., and not 4 o'clock as now. The above were all agreed to.

Some discussion arose out of the proposal of the same committee with respect to the Grand Hotel Slipway. It was subsequently agreed that the Clerk should write to the Lifeboat Institution stating that the Board considered the proposed slipway agreed upon was not the most suitable for the purpose, and that a further plan would be prepared and submitted to the institution.

Mr. Arnott next submitted a scheme for sloping, draining and improving the Marram Cliffs. The estimated cost was £1,500, and the work could be done in sections. Mr. G. Riches thought the suggestion a very sensible one. It would be far better spending that sum of money making the cliffs serviceable to the public than £2,000 on extending the promenade wall seaward.

At present the cliffs were more of a danger than a safeguard to the public. Mr. Curtis – Where is the money to come from to do it? The Board decided to postpone consideration of the scheme until next meeting, the Works Committee in the meantime to visit the site and examine the plan.

Messrs. Jarrold & Son's tender for printing Pier programmes was accepted. Subject to certain conditions, they agreed to supply a maximum of 25,000 copies free, any excess to be paid for at the rate of 3s. per 100. Mr. Curtis asked if any other tenders were sent in. He thought others should have a chance.

The Chairman said they would remember that last year they asked local printers what their terms would be, and Messrs. Jarrold were the only ones who replied, offering to do it then if they were also given the offer this year. But there was no actual pledge. Mr. Curtis – Oh, get out of this year what was lost on last. [Laughter.]

The Chairman said last year only 10,000 copies were supplied; this year there would be 25,000.

On the certificate of the engineer, the following payments were authorised, on the motion of Mr. Puxley, seconded by Mr. Clarke: – Messrs. B. Cooke & Co., repair of retention wall (first certificate), £419;

Mr. A. Thorne, promenade pier £100, pier head shelters £450, and pier superstructure £140.

It was proposed by Mr. Lovelace, seconded by Mr. Curtis, that as recommended by the Finance Committee cheques to the amount of £717 be drawn, including one for £450, third instalment paid for promotion of Protection Act, and £31 15s. legal costs incurred in connection with seven contracts during the year.

The Clerk said their Parliamentary agent's account, £857, was now in, and he thought local costs would be about £300 more, making some £1,150 in all. The costs would be subject to taxation, as would also any sum the Commissioners paid that day. The two previous instalments were £250 and £300 respectively, so that, inclusive of that day's amount, £1,000 would have been paid. The motion was agreed to.

Mr. Gooday, general manager of the G.E.R. Company, having written to the Urban District Council suggesting that any important public function in the town might be made the occasion of inviting a party of London Press men down to write it up, the subject was brought under the notice of the Protection Commissioners at their last meeting.

They then decided to take no notice of it, first, because they had no funds to spend on ceremonies, and, secondly, that they, as the senior public body in the town, had not been first approached.

Second thoughts appear to have proved stronger, and the matter was now considered. Mr. Churchyard thought it would be a "good idea to boom the place."

Mr. Curtis was anxious to know about the cost. Mr. Rogers felt time was important, and to temporise was fatal.

Mr. J. Riches wanted to know what the proposal all meant.

Mr. George Riches felt that the Pier should be "quite" completed before any ceremony took place. Other members were anxious that date of finish should first be known before anything was done. In the end it was decided to reply that the question of an opening ceremony on the finish of the Pier was under consideration, and that when anything further was settled Mr. Gooday should be informed.

It was also resolved to adjourn the meeting until Wednesday next at 2.30 p.m.

Eastern Daily Press: Thursday 11th April 1901

An adjourned meeting of the Cromer Protection Commissioners was held yesterday at the Clerk's Office, Church Street. Mr. A. E. Jarvis presided, and the Press were excluded. The members present were Messrs. R. A. Clarke, H. Rust, A. C. Savin, J. W. Jefferson, L. G. Burton, J. Riches, J. Curtis, and W. Churchyard.

With regard to the proposed "boom", a letter was read from Mr. Gooday, general manager of the G.E.R. Company, intimating their willingness to bear the expense of taking a party of London pressmen to and from Cromer, at the same time suggesting that their entertainment should be done by the town. As the result of private deliberation, the Board settled nothing definite as to an opening ceremony for the Pier, it being as yet impossible to fix a date. They, however, appointed a committee to arrange details and obtain subscriptions if necessary.

East London Advertiser: Saturday 20th April 1901

Now that the sea protection and improvement work at Cromer, which have cost £45,000, are nearing completion, the Commissioners are debating how best to make known the attractions of the town. It is likely that the opening of a new pier will be the occasion of an imposing function.

Eastern Daily Press: Thursday 2nd May 1901

A general meeting was held yesterday at the Clerk's Office, Church Street, Cromer, Mr. A. E. Jarvis in the chair. There were present Messrs. J. Curtis, R. A. Clarke, G. M. Bultitude, J. Bower, A. Burton, J. Riches, F. W. Rogers, G. Riches, A. C. Savin, J. Lovelace, H. Rust, L. G. Burton, T. Puxley and J. W. Jefferson.

The Deputy-Clerk reported the following credit balances in the bank, viz., general account, £525 1s. 5d., and loan ditto, £49 13s. 10d. On the motion of Mr. Clarke, seconded by Mr. Bultitude, payments to the amount of £32 15s. 2d. were confirmed.

The sum included £17 14s. 6d. wage payments made by R. Allen. The Pier receipts for the month were £5 6s. 5d.

The Works Committee recommended that the West Cliff improvement should stand over until the autumn, that in place of the present Bath Hotel breakwater a new one, 150 feet long, should be erected, that an additional hydrant be purchased for the Pier at a cost of £3 15s., that admission to the Pier, hour of closing, and payment of officials be the same as last year, the duties of the officials to begin on 18th May, also that R. Allen be provided with a uniform and given the care of the enclosure on Pier, that the Blue Viennese Band give their first performance on Saturday, 25th May, and that the terms for their playing for the Whitsuntide sports meeting be left with the Chairman to settle, after hearing from Messrs. Keith, Prowse, & Co. on the subject.

Mr. George Riches moved the adoption of the report, with the breakwater recommendation omitted. He thought before anything was done to the Bath Hotel breakwater attention should be given to the Doctor's Steps groyne.

He admitted both were necessary, but considered the eastern one had the prior claim upon them. Mr. H. Rust urged the desirability of giving early attention to the former groyne. Mr. Curtis seconded, and held that the Bath Hotel groyne never was any good. The report was then adopted, and on the motion of Mr. Bower, seconded by Mr. Churchyard, the question of the Bath Hotel groyne was adjourned for a month.

Mr. Curtis proposed, Mr. Puxley seconded, and it was agreed to draw cheques for the following: -

Messrs. B. Cooke & Co. (retaining wall) £264, Messrs. Lewellen & Co. (mains and lighting) £300, Mr. A. Thorne (Pier-head shelters) £300, Mr. A. Thorne (Pier superstructure) £200, Messrs. McDowall & Steven £41 5s., engineer's commission £65 9s., and Mr. A. W. Brown (advertising) £3 0s. 9d.

The Chairman stated that the Pier Opening Committee had held three meetings.

They had been in communication with the G.E.R. Company on the subject, and received a letter from Mr. Gooday, the general manager, that Lord Claud Hamilton (the Chairman) would be pleased to accede to their request to open the Pier if a suitable day could be arranged.

Mr. G. Riches asked how they were to arrive at a definite date, as the Pier was not yet finished.

The Chairman said that in acknowledging Mr. Gooday's letter it was intended to suggest Thursday, 30th May, as the date of the function, should that be convenient to Lord Claud Hamilton.

On the motion of Mr. Bower, seconded by Mr. Puxley, Mr. Alfred Burton was re-appointed collector at the same salary as before. The engineers were instructed to ascertain the Board of Trade requirements as to the light at the Pier-head. The Deputy-Clerk, in reply to Mr. G. Riches, said the Department had been written to as to inspection of the Pier, but no reply had yet been received.

On the motion of Mr. G. Riches, seconded by Mr. Curtis, it was resolved that work on the Doctor's Steps groyne should be gone on with at once. The sum of £900 was authorised to be transferred from the deposit to loan account. The annual meeting of the Board will take place on May 15th.

Downham Market Gazette: Saturday 18th May 1901

PROTECTION COMMISSIONERS. – The annual meeting was held on Wednesday. Mr. A. E. Jarvis was re-elected chairman, and Mr. George Riches vice-chairman.

The Deputy-Clerk reported that Mr. Thomas Fowell Buxton had not attended a meeting of the Board for the last twelve months, and under the Act had ceased to be a Commissioner.

Mr. Curtis asked if they could again nominate him. The Deputy-Clerk replied they could next year, but not this. The Chairman stated that a letter had been received from Mr. Gooday, general manager of the G.E.R. Company, intimating that Saturday, 8th June, and not Thursday, 30th May, would be convenient to Lord Claud Hamilton, chairman of the Company, to open the Pier.

The committee therefore recommended that the ceremony should take place on 8th June. There would be a special train, leaving Liverpool Street at 9.57 a.m., due at Cromer 12.42, and returning at 6.45, arriving in London 9.30 p.m.

The report of the committee was adopted, and it was decided that among those invited should be the following gentlemen, all of whom are ex Commissioners, viz., Sir S. Hoare, Bart., M.P., the Rev. J. F. Sheldon, Mr. H. A. Barclay, Mr. S. Jarvis, Mr. L. G. Burton, and Mr. Isaac Burton.

The Diss Express, and Norfolk and Suffolk Journal: Friday 31st May 1901

At Cromer, the new Pier, now completed, was a great attraction. About 2,000 persons passed the turnstiles during the day. A capital programme of athletic sports was also carried out. The principal event was the N.C.U. Eastern Counties' Centre one mile championship, for which there were five entries, the winner being T. S. Fitch, Norwich A.B.C., who was also the winner of the championship last year.

The Norfolk Chronicle and Norwich Gazette: Saturday 8th June 1901

THE OPENING OF CROMER PIER
COMMISSIONERS' PROGRAMME

A meeting of the Cromer Protection Commissioners was held at the Clerk's Office, Church Street, on Wednesday, Mr. A. E. Jarvis presiding. There were also present Messrs. R. A. Clarke, H. Rust, G. Kennedy, J. B. Hudson, A. C. Savin, J. Bower, F. W. Rogers, F. Barclay, J. W. Jefferson, T. Puxley, W. Churchyard, J. Riches, J. Curtis, G. M. Bultitude, and J. Lovelace. Mr. Arnott (Messrs. Douglass and Arnott, engineers), also attended.

During the month rates to the amount of £9 10s. 5d. had been received by the collector.

Out of a recoverable balance of £22 6s. 7d., there was £15 9s. 11d. due from the Cromer Water Works Company. The secretary wrote that although counsel advised that the reservoir was not rateable under the Protection Act, the sum would be paid under protest, without prejudice as to the future. A letter was also received from the General Post Office in respect to a rate of £5 15s. 5d. for the Post Office premises.

The authorities, in making a contribution towards the total rate of the whole business, claimed exemption from rate for the portion used by them. The Clerk added that since the collector presented his report the remaining balance of the £22 6s. 7d. recoverable rate had been paid.

On the motion of Mr. Curtis, seconded by Mr. Clarke, total wage payments by R. Allen to the amount of £52 0s. 11d. were confirmed.

The Clerk reported that from May 1st to 24th inclusive the pier receipts were £6 2s. 5d.

The Finance Committee, consisting of Messrs. J. Bower, A. E. Jarvis, G. Riches, J. Riches, and H. Rust, were also re-elected en bloc.

The Works Committee reported that in the opinion of the engineers there was no necessity to alter the cutlet holes on the promenade to the west of the pier.

This view, after a protest from Mr. Curtis, the Board confirmed.

They recommended that the east shelter should be painted where necessary, and that the question of the Bath Hotel groyne be considered at the next meeting of the Board; that Mr. A. Thorne's offer to sell a portable forge and other useful goods required by the Board for £12 10s. be accepted; and that the question of the pier awning be left for the consideration of the new Works Committee; that the application of Mr. George Wright for permission to use last year's book of tickets for admission to pier be granted, and that Mr. H. Fox's request to have advertisement leaflets in band programmes be refused.

Mr. Lovelace proposed, and Mr. Curtis seconded, the adoption of the report.

The Chairman said the articles it was proposed to purchase from Mr. Thorne would be most useful, and were of a kind the Commissioners would want sooner or later.

Several tenders had been received for the pier awning. The lowest was about £290.

The report of the committee was then adopted.

Neal, the gatekeeper, having applied for an increase of pay from 17s. to 21s. per week, the Works Committee recommended that from next week to the end of June he should receive 19s., and during July and August 20s. per week.

Mr. Curtis moved an amendment that he be given 20s. a week from next week to the end of August. Mr. Bower seconded, and the amendment was carried.

On the motion of Mr. Clarke, seconded by Mr. Churchyard, the following payments on certificate of the engineers were authorised: – Messrs. B. Cooke and Co. (western section), £1,200 on account of retention money under contract; ditto (Marrams section), £55; and ditto, repairs to retention wall in front of town, £163; total, £1,418. Mr. A. Thorne, pier head shelters, £281; and Messrs. Douglass and Arnott, commission, £53 4s.

It being the time to appoint the Works Committee for the ensuing year, Mr. J. Riches proposed the individual election of members.

Mr. Curtis seconded.

Mr. Rogers moved as an amendment that the members be elected en bloc.

Mr. Churchyard seconded.

The Chairman said he had no personal wish in the matter. At the same time, he desired to say how well the members had worked together and got through a great deal of business.

Mr. Rogers thought that, seeing how the old committee had had all the brunt of the work, it was only fair that they should see to its completion.

On a division, the amendment was carried by eight to seven. The members elected were Messrs. J. Bower, W. Churchyard, A. E. Jarvis, J. Lovelace, G. Riches, F. W. Rogers, and H. Rust.

The Pier Opening Committee reported the completion of arrangements for the opening ceremony (today) Saturday. In accordance with the instructions of the Board, invitations had been limited to the two public bodies in the town, the contractors, and the engineers and their friends, and the railway interests and the Press.

One hundred and twelve invitations had been issued, and up to the present twelve letters of regret had been received.

The Chairman said the programme for the day was as follows: –

The Commissioners and Council will assemble at the Hotel de Paris at one o' clock. Carriages will meet the G.E.R. special due at 12.42, and also those arriving at the Beach Station, and convey the passengers to the above hotel.

The company will then inspect the new promenades and other works, and at 1.30 gather opposite the Pier.

There, Lord Claud Hamilton, chairman of the Great Eastern Railway Company, will be presented with a gold key by the Chairman of the Protection Commissioners for the purpose of opening the pier.

That ceremony over and the pier inspected, the company will proceed to the Hotel de Paris for luncheon at 2.30. Music will there be provided by the Blue Viennese Band, under the conductorship of Herr Moritz Wurm. The band will also perform, and a concert be given, on the pier in the course of the afternoon.

At 4.30, weather permitting, vehicles will be provided for taking those desirous for drives in the neighbourhood, and at 6.15 carriages will convey the visitors to the G.E.R. and Beach Stations.

Mr. Churchyard asked if the M. and G.N. Railway Company had received invitations.

The Chairman replied in the affirmative, and said they had accepted.

The point raised had come before the Opening Committee since the last meeting. It was that twenty-five representatives from various newspapers were coming on the M. and G.N. line, and the railway company's request that two of that number should be invited to the after part of the luncheon to report the proceedings, was acceded to.

Mr. G. Riches did not think that the Board should be one-sided. The G.E.R. were bringing a train load down, and the Board were entertaining them, and the M. and G.N. were bringing others, of whom they were only entertaining two.

The Chairman said that in addition to the 25, the Chairman of the Joint Committee and four or five others had received invitations.

The Clerk added the M. and G.N. were running a luncheon car for their party.

Mr. A. C. Savin said if the M. and G.N. were quite satisfied, well and good. He certainly thought they should treat both companies the same.

The Chairman replied that all that had been asked was granted.

Mr. Churchyard suggested that free admission tickets to the Pier should be given to the M. and G.N. twenty-five. This was agreed to.

Mr. G. Riches asked if the Commissioners had expressed any wish about the decorations.

The Chairman said he thought so far as decorations of the town were concerned, it was far better to have the Pier done well than the town only partially so. The committee, therefore, decided to have the vicinity of the Pier well decorated.

Mr. Riches said he considered that such a decision was rather arbitrary on the whole community. He took it that in the interest of all the inhabitants there was a desire to do the best at decorating the town.

The Chairman replied that there would be no one to prevent their doing it if they so wished.

Mr. G. Riches said he thought Saturday should be a red-letter day in Cromer, and if so, they must put a little spirit into the matter. He thought the decorations would be even better than they were on Mafeking Day.

The subject then dropped, and the meeting adjourned to Wednesday, 26th June, when the rate for the ensuing year will be made.

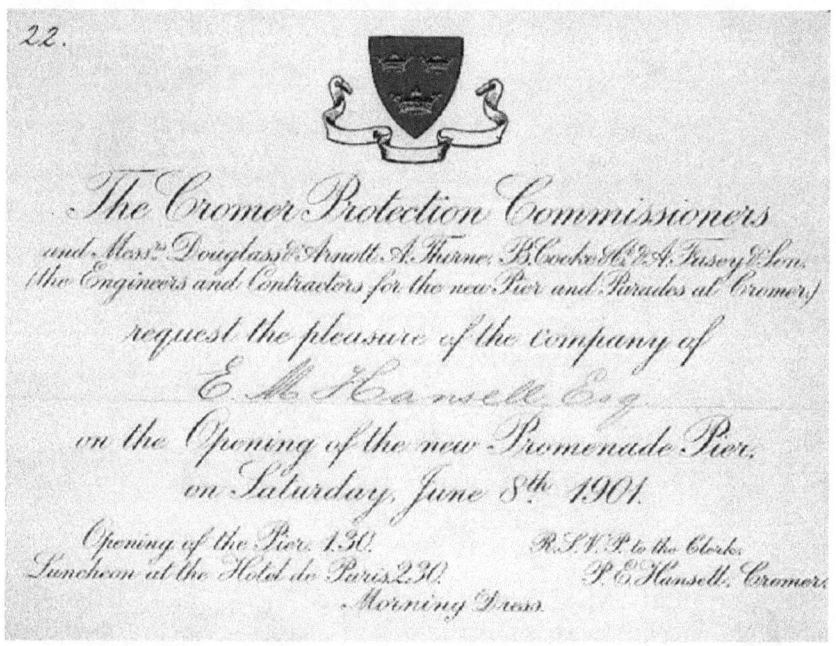

Norfolk Museums Service, Cromer Museum, CRRMU : 1978.36.5
Cromer Pier opening ceremony invitation card

Chapter Six – Official opening day: Saturday 8th June 1901

*Norfolk Museums Service, Cromer Museum, CRRMU : 1981.80.868
Cromer Pier opening ceremony*

Derby Daily Telegraph: Monday 10th June 1901

OPENING OF THE NEW PROMENADE
PIER AT CROMER
(FROM OUR OWN REPORTER)

The pretty little town of Cromer is not so well known in the Midlands as it ought to be, but there is every reason to believe that in the immediate future it will spring into the prominence it so richly deserves.

THE CONSTRUCTION OF CROMER PIER

So much has been written and said of this fashionable watering place that it is perhaps hardly necessary to add that for ocean, cliff, and woodland scenery, Cromer and the country in the immediate vicinity stand almost unrivalled.

Cromer, apart from its local governing authority, is possessed of a body of Commissioners, who are entrusted with the protection of the town from the sea.

It is to the enterprise of this latter authority that the town is now possessed of a promenade pier equal to any in the Kingdom, for when the old jetty was destroyed by the storm which visited the coast in November, 1897, the Commissioners arranged for the erection of a handsome pier.

The latter structure, the first pile of which was driven on January 13th, 1900, has a breadth of 40 feet, with bays extending to 60 feet, and is 500 feet long, while the head, at its extremity, expands to a width of 112 feet, with a symmetrical balancing length of 144 feet.

Shelters, affording comfortable lounges, are placed at frequent intervals along its sides. The great shelter, which includes a bandstand, is at the head of the pier, and can at any time be covered by an awning.

A graceful vestibule, with massive bastions, has been erected at the approach to the pier, and can be reached both by incline and central steps, whilst artistic kiosks have been placed at the entrance.

The pier is constructed of wrought iron piles, driven 20 feet into the bed of the sea, upon which rest cast iron columns carrying steel girders supporting the deck. The new promenade, 1,000 yards in length, with a width of 40 feet, extends from the Lifeboat Station, on the east beach, away beyond the Grand Hotel, on the west beach.

The main portion was completed by the summer season of 1900, while June, 1901, sees the whole works, which in their entirety have cost upwards of £41,000, finished and open to the public.

The contract has been in the hands of Mr. Alfred Thorne, of London.

The resident population of Cromer is estimated at about 4,000, but its death rate is abnormally low, the average for the past three years being 10.5, and for 1900, 8.5 only.

The bathing arrangements are excellent. Boatmen patrol the bathing ground during the season, and every possible precaution is taken for securing the safety of the bathers.

There is plenty of sea fishing and boating to be obtained, and the town is in close proximity to the "Broad" district. Cromer is well served by two railways, viz., those of the Great Eastern and the Midland and Great Northern Joint Companies. The M. and G.N. Joint line has the great advantage of being situated within a few minutes' walk of the beach and new pier; and a special service of trains commencing last Saturday will be run, which will take in Derby during the season.

On Saturday last the town was en fête, the occasion being the opening of the new pier. Special trains were run from all parts, and a large crowd of people were at the pier gates about 1.30.

The opening ceremony was performed by Lord Claud Hamilton, who was supported by Lord De Ramsey, a director of the G.N.R., Mr. H. G. Drury, superintendent of the line of the Great Eastern Railway, Mr. J. J. Petrie, manager of the M. & G.N. Joint Railway, Mr. G. Marsh, assistant secretary, G.N.R., Mr. J. S. Gooday, general manager G.E.R., Mr. Henry Broadhurst, M.P., and others.

Letters of apology had been received from Mr. W. L. Jackson, M.P., and chairman of the G.N.R., Sir G. E. Paget, chairman of the Midland Railway, Mr. C. Steel, general manager G.N.R., Mr. E. W. Wells, assistant general manager Midland Railway, and others.

Lord Claud, before opening the gates, took the opportunity of congratulating the town of Cromer upon the acquisition of such a beautiful pier.

Occasions like these, he said, were not devoted to making public speeches, so he would content himself with formerly declaring the pier open. Lord Claud was accorded a hearty vote of thanks on the motion of Mr. A. E. Jarvis, the chairman of the Cromer Protection Commissioners.

The crowd then followed on the pier, which, like the town itself, presented a very gay appearance with flags, coloured bunting, etc.; and a concert was given in the Great Shelter by the Blue Viennese Band.

THE CONSTRUCTION OF CROMER PIER

Norfolk Museums Service, Cromer Museum, CRRMU : CP4041.16
The pier bandstand – Opening day concert

At the luncheon at the Hotel de Paris, Mr. A. E. Jarvis (Chairman of the Cromer Protection Commissioners) presided. – Lord Claud Hamilton, in proposing "Success to the Cromer Pier, and Prosperity to the Town." referred to his personal acquaintance with Cromer, which dated back some fifty years.

For a great many years, the inhabitants had led a very exclusive life, but eventually a railway found its way to the Norfolk coast.

It was a line which was then known as the East Norfolk Railway, and commenced running trains into the district. Several years later the Midland and Great Northern Railway Companies opened up a line in the district, although the Great Eastern Railway Company did not feel very kindly disposed at this competing venture.

It was, however, felt that the new line would confer a great benefit upon Cromer, and would bring it within touch of the large towns of the Midlands, and the North.

The future of Cromer rested entirely with the inhabitants. They wanted to see the place as select as possible, in fact a high-class seaside resort.

There was no place at Cromer for the day-tripper or the excursionist. It was the desire of the inhabitants to manage the town and its affairs in such a manner as to maintain its present position.

They were determined that the arrangements should be of a high-class character, and that the place should be made suitable for those who required a rest. (Hear, hear.)

The Chairman, in responding to the toast, spoke in very eulogistic terms of the advantages of Cromer as a healthy seaside resort.

Other toasts followed, and included "The Chairman," "Lord Claud Hamilton," and "The Railway Interests."

The latter toast was submitted by Mr. Henry Broadhurst, M.P., and was responded to by Lord De Ramsey (Director of the G.N. Railway Co.).

Eastern Daily Press: Monday 10th June 1901

THE IMPROVEMENT OF
CROMER
OPENING THE NEW PIER
SPEECH BY LORD C. HAMILTON

Time was when the people of Cromer regarded with aversion the very idea of doing anything to add to the attractiveness of their town, believing that the natural beauties of the place were quite sufficient to draw such visitors as were desired by this exclusive little seaside resort.

Of late, however, more progressive ideas have prevailed, and Cromer has taken its first step in advance by erecting a Pier and engaging a first-class band to play thereon daily during the season.

The Pier – which takes the place of the old Jetty destroyed by a storm in 1897 – and the promenade – which serves the double purpose of

THE CONSTRUCTION OF CROMER PIER

protecting the coast from the incursions of the sea and of affording a pleasant stroll to visitors – have already been described in these columns, and it only remains for us to deal with the opening ceremony which took place on Saturday.

Much as Cromer dislikes publicity, the Commissioners were induced to allow the railway companies serving the town – the Great Eastern and the Midland and Great Northern Joint Committee – to bring down a great crowd of newspaper men who will make the beauties of the place known all over England.

The G.E.R. ran a special train from London with some sixty journalists and others on board, drawn chiefly from the Metropolis, and the Midland and Great Northern tapped the Midland counties. The specials reached Cromer shortly before one o'clock, and the visitors immediately afterwards gathered in front of the Hotel de Paris, which faces the Pier.

The inaugural ceremony took place in brilliant weather, and Cromer looked at its best. To mark the event quite a liberal display of bunting had been made on the Pier and the Parade, and in the town, flags were flying in all directions. The zig-zag staircases up the side of the cliff were packed with gaily dressed ladies, and altogether the scene was a bright and pleasing one, as the local bodies, the high officials of the railway companies, and the journalists gathered in front of the closed gates of the Pier. The ceremony was a brief one.

Lord Claud Hamilton, chairman of the Great Eastern Railway Company, addressing the gathering said: – It will be appropriate before opening the Pier for me to make one or two observations.

In the first place I wish to express my acknowledgement to the members of the Cromer Protection Commission for asking me to perform the inaugural ceremony; and in the second place I desire to congratulate the people of Cromer on the public spirit they have exhibited in erecting, through the medium of the Commissioners, this beautiful parade and promenade, a part of which we have just traversed, and this excellent and picturesque Pier, the gates of which I am about to open.

THE CONSTRUCTION OF CROMER PIER

I confess when I look upon this new and beautiful edifice my thoughts fly back to the dear old jetty which I know and remember for 30 years. It is of no use regretting what no longer exists, but I think the oldest inhabitants of Cromer will have the satisfaction of feeling that the old jetty, which they regarded with such veneration, was finally removed, not by the hand of man, but by the irresistible forces of nature.

Mr. Jarvis and gentlemen, having said these few words, I beg to declare the pier open [Cheers.]

Mr. Jarvis, chairman of the Board, then said he had on behalf of the Cromer Protection Commissioners to thank Lord Claud for the very great interest he had taken in the opening of the Pier and in coming down to perform the ceremony.

To judge by the numbers present there was no doubt the pier would be one of the greatest attractions in the future.

He then asked Lord Claud on behalf of the Board to accept the gold key with which to perform the opening ceremony.

His lordship then formally opened the Pier, and as the party went on, the Blue Viennese Band played the National Anthem.

The key was supplied by Elkington & Co., 73, Cheapside, London. It is of elaborate repoussé work. On one side of the head, it bears the seal of the Board and round it the words, "Cromer Protection Commission, 1845, incorporated under new Act, 1899." On the other side is Lord Claud Hamilton's monogram, surmounted by a coronet. The inscription on the other part of the key is, "Cromer Protection Commissioners. With this key Lord Claud Hamilton opened the new promenade pier at Cromer, on June 8th, 1901."

Half an hour was spent on the Pier listening to the excellent playing of the Blue Viennese Band, under Herr Moritz Wurm, and then the company retired and the gates were thrown open to the public free of charge. They gladly availed themselves of the privilege, and soon the pier was packed. All admired its beautiful proportions and its many arrangements for the comfort and pleasure of visitors.

LUNCHEON AT THE HOTEL DE PARIS

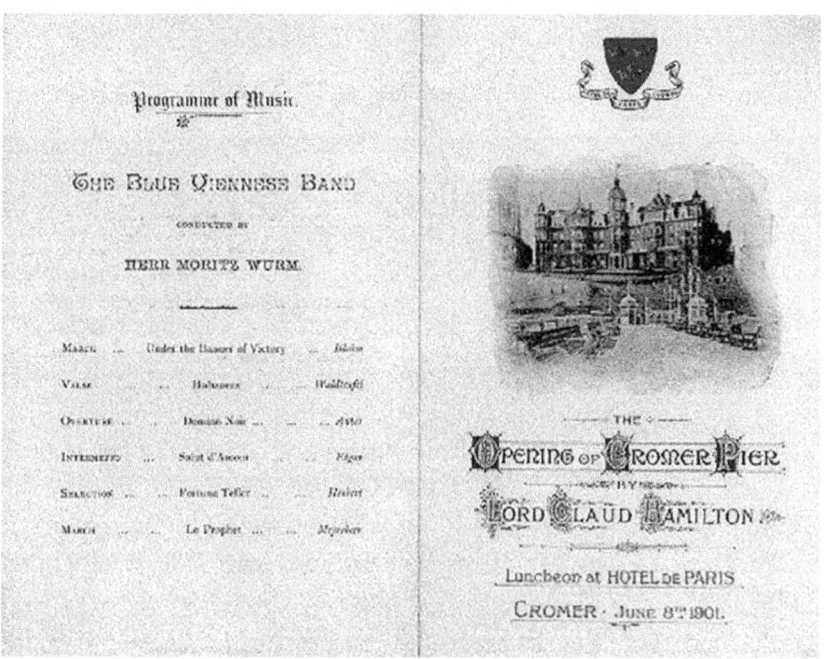

Norfolk Museums Service, Cromer Museum, CRRMU : 1978.36.6a
Programme of music

At half-past two, on the invitation of the Cromer Protection Commissioners and Messrs. Douglass and Arnott, A. Thorne, B. Cooke & Co., and A. Fasey & Son (the engineers and contractors for the new Pier and parades), a large company sat down to luncheon at the Hotel de Paris.

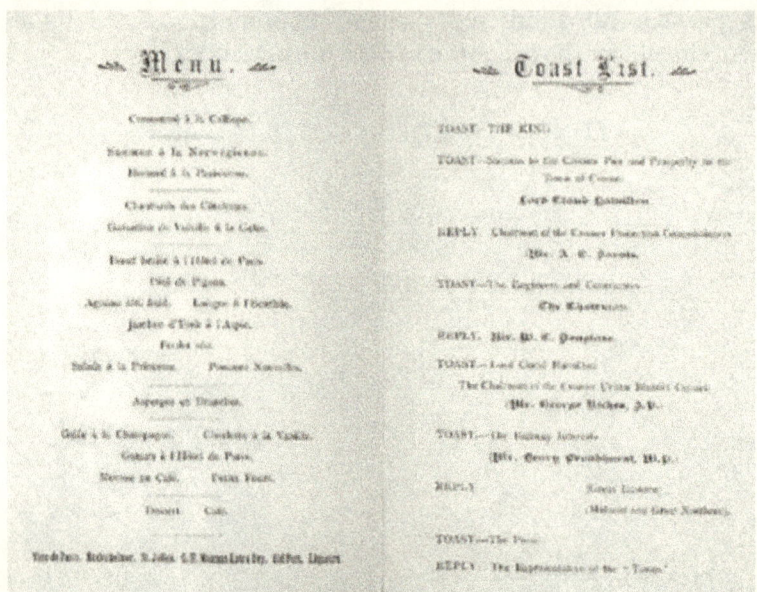

*Norfolk Museums Service, Cromer Museum, CRRMU : 1978.36.6a
Menu and toast list*

There were six toasts. Mr. Jarvis, who presided, gave "The Health of the King."

Lord Claud Hamilton, in proposing "Success to the Cromer Pier and Prosperity to the Town of Cromer," said he had known Cromer personally or by reputation for the past fifty years. It was his good fortune to be at a private school with Sir Samuel Hoare and his late lamented brother, and also with several members of the Buxton family, who at that remote period used to reside at Cromer.

He remembered well how his mouth used to water at the accounts by his youthful schoolfellows of the masses of amber and jet they used to pick up on the Beach at Cromer.

He longed to emulate them, but he learned that Cromer at that period of its history was an almost inaccessible spot. He understood that it was entirely inhabited by Gurneys and Buxtons and Hoares and wild parrots. [Laughter.]

The former had become greatly reduced in number, while the latter had entirely disappeared. He was sorry to trace these results to what was vulgarly termed railway enterprise. In those days the inhabitants of Cromer jealously guarded the rights they possessed and resented any intrusion upon their privacy.

Consequently, the railway promoters of that period found it exceedingly difficult to penetrate to the coast of Norfolk anywhere in the neighbourhood of Cromer.

But after all public interest in these days must overcome private desire for seclusion, and in spite of all opposition a railway called the East Norfolk Railway finally found its way to Cromer.

One of the results of the opposition which that project received from the inhabitants of Cromer was that the terminus of the railway was in a place that was a somewhat inconvenient location. It might be termed a monumental station situate like a statue on the very summit of an eminence instead of being on a level. That, after all, had its merits, for it presented visitors on their arrival at Cromer with a view that was unequalled by any to be seen from any other railway station in the kingdom.

Looking down upon the town of Cromer cosily nestling below them, with light hearts visitors commenced the descent. After spending a few hours in the heat of the sun at Cromer, the necessity came upon trippers to return to their very elevated station, and they would then speedily find that a very different tale was told.

On many occasions he had witnessed working people plodding back gasping for breath, the wives saying, "Oh, Bill, won't you give us a help with the baby!" as a result of the heavy gradient to the station.

It was no fault of the G.E.R. that the station was on so elevated a spot, and it would have to remain where it was. All the G.E.R. could do was to give Cromer a quick and punctual service.

That they had endeavoured to do, and he believed they had succeeded. In the old days the G.E.R. was the only railway that served Cromer and it viewed with jealousy the approach of any competitors; but fortunately, wiser and better counsels prevailed.

The G.E.R. now felt that while they could reasonably convey those who wished to visit Cromer from the Metropolis with greater facility than any other company, there were other districts in the United Kingdom the inhabitants of which might wish to visit Cromer for whom the G.E.R. could not offer the same facilities that might be afforded by other railway companies; and though the competition of the Midland and Great Northern Joint Committee was at first a little bit feared by the G.E.R., they now recognised that it had done them no harm, and had certainly been of great advantage to Cromer.

While the G.E.R. gave the best and most speedy access from the Metropolis, the Midland and Great Northern gave access to towns in the midland and northern counties which the G.E.R. could not do. The result had been that a large number of people had been brought to Cromer, and the G.E.R. had not suffered in any way.

The future of Cromer rested very much with the people themselves. He hoped the G.E.R. would never be asked to make Cromer a cheap trippers' resort. [Hear, hear.]

Railway companies were very much ruled by the desires of the localities they served.

Although he admitted that under certain circumstances cheap trippers were a very desirable element in certain places, he did honestly feel that Cromer was not a place where one could invite cheap trippers from all parts of the kingdom. [Hear, hear.]

Norwich and the large towns in Norfolk had a right to ask the railway companies to take them to the seaside resorts in their own county at a reasonable charge, but it was difficult with the cheap trippers from the Metropolis and the towns in the Midlands who, from the nature of their amusements and tastes, did not add to the amenities or the dignity of a seaside place.

He had a great belief in the future of Cromer, and he hoped it would maintain its present dignity. A great deal would depend upon the class of buildings they erected.

They did not want the jerry builder in Cromer, but they wanted nice buildings with nice gardens. Whatever other towns in the district might do – and there were towns that welcomed the London cheap tripper – he advised Cromer in its own interest to maintain its partial exclusiveness and to cater only for those who were in the better paths of life. [Hear, hear.]

Mr. Jarvis in responding, said that during the past three years the death rate of Cromer had been 10.5 per thousand, and during the past year only 8.5 per thousand. This was a little bit out of the ordinary run, and spoke volumes for the health of the place. The scenery around Cromer compared favourably with that of any seaside place. In most places there were only about three drives to be taken; but in Cromer it was possible to take a fresh drive every day for a fortnight.

With regard to the work that had been carried out by the Protection Commissioners, they had had to contend with difficulties from the very commencement. Before they could sign the contract, they had to obtain a special Act of Parliament which met with opposition from various quarters.

Then when the work was begun, the foundations were washed away four times.

The sea also smashed the pile-driving engine, and washed away the staging. In spite of all these difficulties Cromer could now boast of having one of the finest and prettiest little piers to be found anywhere.

They were told that a pier would spoil Cromer, but the Commissioners thought otherwise. He knew a great many seaside resorts, but he did not know a single place where the visitors, taken as a whole, were of such a good class as those to be found at Cromer.

Bearing this in mind the Commissioners embedded in their scheme all the best points of other piers, and carefully excluded everything that would lower the tone of the place. They would not find any trade advertisements, or automatic machines, or drinking bars, or shops on the Cromer Pier.

At the head of the Pier, shelters were arranged in such a way that, no matter which way the wind blew, it was possible to get out of it, and at the same time to enjoy the sunshine and obtain the benefit of the air for which Cromer was celebrated.

Inside the enclosure there would be no fourth or fifth rate theatrical performances, but a really good band. He thought the works reflected very great credit on the engineer and the contractors, and he begged to propose their health.

Mr. W. T. Douglass, in responding, expressed the pleasure he and his firm had experienced in carrying out the work, and said how sorry he would be to leave Cromer.

THE CONSTRUCTION OF CROMER PIER

The operations were started in the latter part of 1899. Very great difficulties had to be contended with during the winter months, but all the works were carried out within the specified time.

The G.E.R. had shown what they could do in bringing men down from London in 2¾ hours. He looked forward to a continuance of those fast trains, in which event the Commissioners would have to extend their promenade to the second mile stone.

Mr. George Riches (Chairman of the Cromer Urban District Council) gave the health of Lord Claud Hamilton.

Lord Claud Hamilton said it had been a source of unmitigated pleasure to him to come to Cromer to perform the duties they had imposed upon him.

Many of those present were not aware how long he had been connected with their charming town. It was 30 years since he was first elected a member for King's Lynn, and shortly after that he went to Cromer to spend a weekend. The then much respected rector, Mr. Fitch – [Hear, hear] – was ill, and he (Lord Claud) read the Lessons in church for him. [Hear, hear.]

When the Felbrigg estate was on the market in 1850 his late father, the Duke of Abercorn, inspected it with a view to purchase, but he said the distance from Norwich was too great, for it involved a drive, and the service by that horrid line, the G.E.R. was so abominable that it would be a degradation for him to have to travel by such a line. [Laughter.] At that time the noble Duke's son had not joined the directorate of the G.E.R. [Laughter.]

Mr. Henry Broadhurst, M.P., proposed "The Railway Interest." He said there were few people who did more railway travelling than he. His average was more than 25,000 miles a year on main lines. This showed that he had had some experience of railway management and railway arrangements.

He was deeply indebted to the railway companies for having carried him so many years over so many miles so safely and so comfortably. The town of Cromer was greatly indebted to the G.E.R. and to the Midland and Great Northern Joint Committee – and might he also incidentally say that those companies were also deeply indebted to the town of Cromer for affording them an opening for their ventures. [Laughter.]

There was no corner of Great Britain that offered such magnificent temptations to railway enterprise as the district of Cromer, which was well known through the world as an earthly paradise. [Laughter.]

Mr. Jarvis had said that a visitor could take a fresh drive every day for a fortnight, but really a lifetime would not suffice for the exploration of all the beauties of the neighbourhood. Within six or seven miles there were the remains of an old castle, which he believed Queen Bess used to visit on a bicycle – [Laughter] – and which was defended against the combined forces of the world by Lady Paston, who frightened the universe on a motor car. [Laughter.]

Everybody grumbled at railways. They were like a certain party in the State of whom a great wit wrote that while most people had many faults, they had but two – "There's nothing right they say, there's nothing right they do." [Laughter.]

He did not agree with that. He was old enough to remember the days when railways were few and far between, and quite inaccessible to the poor.

All that was changed now. The G.E.R. gave facilities second to none in England for reaching the east coast of Norfolk.

The enormous advance Cromer had made was shown by some post-office statistics.

He remembered when the post-office staff consisted of 17 persons, to-day it consisted of 40. At that time, in one week in August, 11,712 letters were dispatched and received. At last Christmas the number had increased to 68,953.

The telegrams in the month of August in 1880 amounted to 3,340; last year to 14,000. In 1880 there were seven mails in and out; in 1900 there were thirty, thanks to the G.E.R. and the M. and G.N. Joint.

In 1880 there were only two deliveries in Cromer; in 1900 there were four. He ventured to say there was no place on the whole of the coast of Great Britain that had shown a more marvellous increase and a more solid development than the town of Cromer.

Mr. Gooday responded on behalf of the G.E.R., remarking that in 1877 his company took 3,000 passengers to Cromer, and in 1900, 21,000.

Lord De Ramsey replying on behalf of the Midland and Great Northern Joint Committee, said he had lived within sight of the hills over Cromer for fifty-two years, and he had attended that function not only as representing the M. and G.N. Railway, but as a friend and neighbour and a Norfolk man who, putting aside railways altogether, was delighted to see his nearest seaside town thriving, increasing, and flourishing. [Hear, hear.]

He desired at once to reciprocate the most friendly feeling in which Lord Claud had referred to the Joint Railway. He passed by Mr. Gooday's remarks as being more adapted to the keen competition of the staffs, especially as directors had to think of policy rather than of whether a train was half an hour late.

To show what a delusion it was that railway companies hated each other, let him refer to what had been done quite recently on the east coast.

To avoid litigation and unnecessary bother and expenditure the M. and G.N. had welcomed the G.E.R. into one of their plums in the shape of Sheringham, and the G.E.R. had admitted the M. and G.N. into one of their plums in the shape of Lowestoft.

Surely that was good for the public at large and for the shareholders of the railway companies.

There was nothing that hampered railway directors so much as the constant Parliamentary interference that they suffered from. If Parliament would give them a free hand to deal with the public safety as they thought best they would be able to serve both the public and the shareholders better.

The old pier had gone and the old coach had gone. Now there was a new Pier, and there were competing railways. Who could tell what was going to happen.

It was refreshing to those who were thinking of the possibilities of railway enterprise to see that the rateable value of Cromer had increased threefold in ten years. He hoped that if the railway companies brought more people to Cromer, the Cromer people would see to it that there was plenty of accommodation for them.

The Midland and Great Northern had made up their minds to stick to this happy corner, and he believed nobody would be the worse for it. He pleaded for time.

The company could not do everything at once, but when they had had time to double the line from Peterborough to Cromer there would be no cause for fault-finding with the service.

He could quite understand that they would like to keep that nice corner select and secluded, but they must remember that out of every 100 persons who travelled, 95 went third class, and it was for them to consider whether it was right or wrong for them to assist in a policy that deterred the working classes from seeing the coast, and whether it would not be advisable to assist that fine old British institution, the excursionist, to come to Cromer. It was an open question, and he expressed no opinion upon it.

Mr. Jarvis proposed the toast of the "Press," and Mr. Richardson (Daily Telegraph) and Mr. Jones (Norfolk Chronicle) responded.

During the luncheon the Blue Viennese Band played selections of music.

Subsequently many of the guests were taken for drives round the district, and later in the evening the visitors from London returned in a G.E.R. special, dinner being provided by the directors on board the train.

THE M. AND G.N. DINNER AT THE HOTEL METROPOLE

In connection with the opening of the Pier, the Midland and Great Northern Joint Committee ran a special dining car train from London, conveying a party of visitors to take part in the ceremony.

The train, which left King's Cross at 8.45 a.m., arrived at Beach Station at 12.40 p.m. In addition to Lord De Ramsey (Director), Mr. J. J. Petrie (Traffic Manager), Mr. Geo. Mason (Assistant-Superintendent, G.N.R.), Mr. H. W. Dixon (Advertising Department, King's Cross), there was a large party of Pressmen from London and the chief Midland and northern towns served by the company, including Birmingham, Nottingham, Derby, Sheffield, Leeds, and Bradford.

At the conclusion of the inaugural ceremony on the Pier the Pressmen were entertained by the company to a most sumptuous luncheon at the Hotel Metropole.

The floral decorations of the table were exquisite, and the party, which numbered forty-three all told, were able to enjoy a magnificent sea view from the windows of the room where they were assembled.

Mr. George Mason (Assistant-Superintendent, G.N.R.) presided in the absence of Mr. J. J. Petrie, who was at the Hotel de Paris. There were also present Mr. H. W. Dixon (Advertising Department, King's Cross), Mr. W. Newman (Assistant Locomotive Superintendent, M. and G.N. Joint Line) and the Station Master of Cromer Beach station.

At the conclusion of the repast, "The Health of the M. and G.N. Company" was given by Mr. McClelland of Sketch.

On behalf of the gathering, he thanked them heartily for the courtesy extended to the Press in attending the interesting function of the day and for the pleasure given them. The toast was drunk with enthusiasm.

Mr. Mason, in reply, said he was pleased to have had such a party, and hoped they had all enjoyed their journey. He was sorry Mr. Petrie was unable to join them, but he had been called to the other table. He wished them all a pleasant return home.

Carriages, supplied by Mr. G. W. Wilkin, the company's local agent, then conveyed members of the party for a pleasant drive in the neighbourhood, Felbrigg Park and the Roman Encampment being visited.

All the guests were given a very tastefully arranged booklet descriptive of the recent improvements in Cromer. The return journey was made at six o'clock from the Beach Station.

The Morning Leader (London): Wednesday 12th June 1901

The Kentish Mercury: Friday 14th June 1901

..... The day was rendered further memorable by the fact that the Great Eastern made a record journey. The train conveying directors and officials of the company travelled from Liverpool Street to Cromer in two hours and forty minutes, which is nearly twenty minutes faster than any train has yet covered the distance. The return journey was accomplished in one minute less.

The Bradford Weekly Telegraph: Saturday 15th June 1901

Cromer is just now in high favour with well to do holiday makers. The Protection Commissioners and the railway companies are taking care that the public shall hear of the beauties of Poppyland and receive a pressing invitation to visit those hospitable shores.

Mr. Henry Broadhurst, M.P., who was in Bradford the other week, is one of the great eulogists of Cromer. He said at a luncheon on Saturday that you might find a fresh drive every day for ten years.

Certainly, the country round the coast is charming, with undulating hills, clothed with oak and birch.

At every winding of the road, you get a glimpse of the sea or the roofs of Sheringham and the other watering-places which outline the coast as far as the eye can reach.

Cromer is the centre of a great golfing district. The hills around are dotted with the bright uniforms of the golfers, while the club houses are marvels of luxury.

With golf, the resinous air from the pines, a place "Where every prospect pleases," this coast ought surely to be irresistible in its attractions.

The occasion of our visit on Saturday was the opening of the new pier. This structure is not as long as Southend, nor so crowded with popular features as Blackpool.

It is a comparatively modest structure of 500 ft. long, while the great bay at the end containing the bandstand is 112 feet broad and 144 feet long.

The Commissioners, it is said, declined to extend the pier far into deep water lest the day tripper should choose to descend in its thousands upon this peaceful reservation.

The other improvements include a fine promenade stretching from the lifeboat station on the east beach and past the Grand Hotel on the west beach.

The Illustrated London News: Saturday 15th June 1901

NEW PIER AT CROMER, OPENED ON JUNE 8 BY LORD CLAUD HAMILTON.

THE CONSTRUCTION OF CROMER PIER

The Sketch: Wednesday 19th June 1901

Acknowledgements

I would like to thank my Mum and Dad for their support and encouragement and could never have imagined that what started as a hobby would evolve into a published reference book.

I have enjoyed researching this era of Cromer's history and it would be nice to think that someone will revisit and expand this work to include information from other sources at a future time.

I would also like to thank the staff of the Norfolk Museums Service, the Mary Evans Picture Library and the British Newspaper Archive for their help, advice and guidance. It was a pleasure to correspond with you all.

––––

The following content was provided by THE BRITISH LIBRARY BOARD. ALL RIGHTS RESERVED. With thanks to The British Newspaper Archive (www.britishnewspaperarchive.co.uk).

Eastern Daily Press: Tuesday 21st December 1897
The Norfolk Chronicle and Norwich Gazette: Saturday 10th June 1899
Supplement to the Norwich Mercury: Saturday 22nd July 1899
Eastern Daily Press: Monday 23rd October 1899
Eastern Daily Press: Thursday 1st February 1900
Eastern Daily Press: Friday 8th June 1900
The Morning Leader (London): Wednesday 12th June 1901

––––

The following content was provided by the Mary Evans Picture Library:

The Sketch: Wednesday 1st August 1900
The Sphere: Saturday 11th August 1900 (Back cover image)
The Illustrated London News: Saturday 15th June 1901
The Illustrated Sporting and Dramatic News: Saturday 15th June 1901
The Sketch: Wednesday 19th June 1901

© Illustrated London News Ltd. / Mary Evans Picture Library

THE CONSTRUCTION OF CROMER PIER

I think it fitting that the last page of the book should be dedicated to the Cromer Protection Commissioners, their engineer, Mr. William Tregarthen Douglass and everyone else involved in the design and construction of Cromer's Promenade Pier.

Norfolk Museums Service, Cromer Museum, CRRMU : 1986.8.85
Cromer Protection Commissioners

Thanks guys